Stefan Wischner
Marjolein Hoekstra

OneNote Secrets

100 Tips & Tricks

for OneNote 2013 & 2016

3rd Edition
2016

OneNote Secrets
3rd Edition Aug 2016

Publisher:

Stefan Wischner
Rebensdorf 10 1/3
84144 Geisenhausen
Germany

Editing: Nadine Caplette

Title: Norbert Maier

Print: CreateSpace

© 2016 Stefan Wischner, Marjolein Hoekstra

Table of Contents

Introduction

It's a little odd. There's hardly a Microsoft program that is as useful, underestimated and, at the same time, as poorly documented as OneNote. Even after many years of intensive use I am still discovering subtleties and strangeness, deficiencies and ingenuities.

This book is a collection of many of my personal discoveries about OneNote 2010, 2013 and 2016. Most are just too good and useful to keep them to myself.

This is not a complete documentation or handbook for OneNote 2013 / 2016. Instead it's a more or less loose collection of tips, hints and how-tos. It's in the nature of tip compilations that, most likely, not every single tip will be of particular interest to you. But I am quite sure you will discover a lot of things you didn't know. It may even be that one or two of the tips will provide you with the solution to an actual problem or answer a question nobody else could answer.

There is a loose organization in chapters covering certain topics like the OneNote editor or organizing your notes, but inside those chapters there is no particular order. Just browse!

A note for Windows tablet users

Tablet computers with a regular Windows operating system on it (like the Microsoft Surface series) can run the full desktop versions of MS Office 2013 or 2016. This includes the Office-version of OneNote 2013/2016 as well as the free OneNote 2016 from **www.onenote.com**.

Note: This is not to be confused with the OneNote tablet app which is pre-installed on Windows 10. More about that in the next section.

Therefore, almost all of the tips in this book work for OneNote 2013/2016 on tablets as well. However, this book will tend to use desktop oriented terms, such as keyboard shortcuts and mouse actions. In many cases tablet users can replace the word "click" with "touch" or "tap on". There are some differences when using your finger. To open a context menu, for example, you may have to "tap and hold" instead of "right-clicking".

What about the other OneNote versions?

This book is all about the Windows desktop versions OneNote 2013 and OneNote 2016. Since the introduction of Windows 8 there has been an additional tablet-optimized version of One-Note. This "Metro" or "Modern UI" App can be downloaded from the Microsoft store for free. Windows 10 comes with a pre-installed updated version - now called OneNote "Store App" or "Universal App". You can easily distinguish the tablet app from the "full" OneNote 2013/2016: Its icon in the Windows start menu is just named "OneNote" without any version number. The Universal App may access and use the same notebooks as the desktop versions, as long as they are stored on OneDrive, but in comparison to the desktop versions of OneNote, a lot of features are missing. Similar restrictions apply to OneNote for iOS, Android, Windows 8/10 Mobile, Mac and OneNote Online. Most tips in this book won't work with those versions.

OneNote 2013 vs. OneNote 2016

You may have noticed that the title of this book is addressing OneNote 2013 and 2016 at the same time. How is that possible?

The reason is simple: The upgrade from OneNote 2013 to 2016 brought hardly any changes to the program. Both versions are almost identical. So all tips and instructions in this book are valid for both versions. This includes the Onetastic Add On and its macro language. Most screenshots in this book are from One-Note 2016 but, apart from the color of the menu bar, you will notice no differences at all.

I said "almost identical" before. So, exactly what are the differences between OneNote 2013 and 2016? Just these:

- In OneNote 2013 you may import a picture or document directly from the scanner. That function has been completely removed in OneNote 2016. According to Microsoft the reason has been a general instability especially with the 64-Bit versions of Office. True reason? Doesn't matter, that feature is gone.

- In OneNote 2013 all menu labels have been written in capital letters (eg. *INSERT*). OneNote 2016 reverted them to regular writing (*Insert*).

- A new color scheme has been added. It's called "colorful" and changes the windows title bar to OneNote-purple. You may change the color scheme by navigating to *File – Options – General*.

- The Backstage view (*File* Menu) has been slightly modified. The list of recently opened notebooks is now grouped and sorted in chronological order.

- Since OneNote 2016 build number 16.0.6366.2036 it is possible to insert certain live content into notes, for example, video clips from YouTube or Vimeo.
- The separate OneNote Tool for screen clippings or quick notes no longer has its own window. It is now located in the system tray. The *Send to OneNote* command has been removed and the keyboard shortcut for quick notes has changed to **[Win] + [N]**. In OneNote 2013 you had to press **[N]** twice.

That's about all for now (Aug 2016). New features may be added to OneNote 2016 in the future. It is very likely though that only subscribers of Office 365 (with a subscription plan that includes Office 2016 licenses) will get new features.

OneNote 2016 (Office) vs. 2016 (free)

In March 2016 Microsoft surprised users with the announcement that the full OneNote 2013 for Windows could be downloaded and installed for free.

A closer look quickly revealed that this was not the exact truth. In fact, that free version of OneNote 2013 lacked a lot of features compared with the version that comes with MS Office 2013.

Microsoft added most of the missing features like password protecting sections or recording audio notes with the following updates. Now the free OneNote 2016 (the 2013 version has been abandoned) comes rather close to the Office version. A few restrictions remain though and it's very likely that this will not be changed:

- **No locally stored notebooks**. The free version of OneNote 2016 requires notes to be saved on OneDrive or OneDrive for Business. Local drives or network shares are only supported by those OneNote 2013/2016 versions that come with Office 2016 / Office 365. Also there are some restrictions importing ONE- and ONEPKG files (there is more information about this later in this book).

- No "visual embedding" of Excel worksheets or Visio-Documents. They may just be stored as link or embedded files like any other file format.

- Notes cannot be exported in DOC or DOCX formats. To do this some DLL files would be needed that are part of the complete Office 2016.

- No interaction with **MS Outlook** (like exchanging ToDo lists). That should not be a problem though; usually users of Outlook do own the complete MS Office suite and as such the full featured OneNote as well.

Apart from these restrictions the free and Office-OneNote 2013/2016 are pretty much identical. So most of the tips in this book are valid for both versions. The few exceptions will be clearly marked.

Now let's get straight to the tips. We hope you enjoy rummaging and browsing and hopefully find something which is really useful to you.

Chapter 1   **Tips about the Editor**

Although the Editor of OneNote 2013 and 2016 does seem a lot like Microsoft Word, it is different in many ways. This chapter is all about entering, editing and formatting OneNote content.

1 Deactivating the grid

Every time you move objects such as pictures, shapes or containers inside a OneNote page, they automatically snap to an invisible grid. To have precise control over the exact position of objects on a page, just press and hold the **[Alt]** key to move the objects freely.

To make the grid visible, open the menu from *View – Rule Lines* and select the leftmost grid under *Grid Lines*.

You may also switch off the *Snap to Grid* feature permanently. The corresponding command is somewhat hidden: Open the *Draw* menu and click on the small *More*-symbol (a triangle pointing downwards with a horizontal line above it). It's located in the lower-right corner of the *Shapes* gallery. That opens a pull-down menu. Click on the entry *Snap to Grid* to deactivate the grid permanently. Do the same to turn it on again.

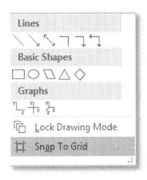

2 Accurate positioning using the keyboard

In the last tip we showed you how to switch the invisible grid off. But maybe you need an accurate positioning just occasionally. Unlike most graphics software, OneNote doesn't offer a dedicated function to move objects by pressing an additional key. For containers and for images positioned directly on the OneNote canvas, you can use the following workaround:

1. Select the whole object frame. Alternatively place the cursor somewhere inside the frame and press **[Ctrl]+[A]** multiple times as needed.

2. Open the context menu (right-click or **[Shift]** + **[F10]**).

3. Select the *Move* command from the menu or press **[M]**.

4. Now you may move the frame using the cursor keys. Press and hold the **[Ctrl]** key for a pixel-by-pixel movement.

In a similar fashion, you can use the keyboard for resizing. Step 3 will then be to select the *Resize* command from the object context menu.

3 Splitting and merging containers

One of the nice things about OneNote is that it makes it very easy to position content anywhere on the page. If you later decide that you want to organize that content in a different way, by splitting or merging containers, that too is no problem.

Splitting containers

Sometimes you may want to pull out content from a frame (container) and place it into a new container, for example to move that content somewhere else on the page. There are two ways to do this:

Method 1: Select all content that you want to move, then press-and-hold the left mouse button and drag the selection to a new position on the page.

Method 2: The *Insert space* command, located on the *Draw* menu, is intended to create space between containers. It's also possible to use it to split an existing (text) container horizontally into two containers.

Caution: The cut extends over the whole page width. Any content located to the left or right of the actual frame gets split as well.

Merging containers

The reverse operation is useful too; combining the contents of two containers into one container. This is a seamless process.

1. Point your mouse cursor to the quadruple-dot title bar of the source container. A four-sided mouse cursor will appear.
2. **[Shift]** + Left-click on that container bar. Keep your mouse button pressed and drag & drop the source container into the destination container. When the two containers snap, they are automatically merged.

While dragging and dropping, you can keep your mouse button pressed even longer to determine the exact location in the target container where the contents of the source container is to be inserted.

When splitting or merging containers, you can select multiple individual text paragraphs and other objects by holding the **[Ctrl]**-key down and clicking on those objects' paragraph marks in the margin.

The exact same procedures can be used to drag an image away from an existing container and onto the page canvas. The reverse works too: You can drag an image from the canvas onto a container.

4 Inserting space horizontally and vertically

If you need additional free space between existing objects you may use the *Insert Space* function found on the *Insert* menu. A horizontal line will appear with a double-pointed mouse arrow. You can now click and drag this arrow downwards to insert space. Less known is the fact that you may use this feature to push content sideways as well.

After clicking on *Insert Space*, just move the mouse pointer to the left margin of the page until the mouse pointer changes to a vertical line with an arrow pointing to the right. Now push existing content sideways by clicking and dragging the mouse cursor in that direction. This also works in the opposite direction: From the page margin on the far right, you can push existing content to the left.

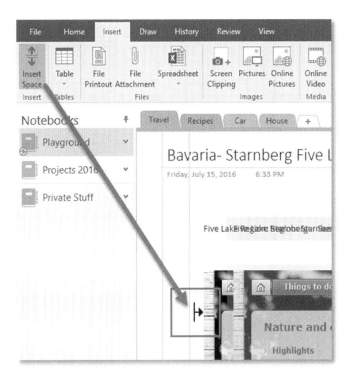

Note that you are limited to inserting space starting from the left page margin and moving inward. You cannot create space vertically from the middle of a page. *Insert Space* affects objects both inside and outside of a container. See also the Splitting Containers tip (page 16) for a different way to use the *Insert Space* command.

To create additional writing space at the end of the page there's another method: Simply scroll to the bottom of the page and click on the scroll bar's down arrow to append some extra lines. Repeat as needed.

5 Limiting the page size

OneNote's unlimited canvas is one of its unique features – but sometimes an unwanted one. Especially when it comes to printing, page contents may be wildly spread over several sheets of paper. You can only avoid that by repeatedly resizing all content and controlling the print preview. Also, browsing through a page to find specific information can be a pain if you have to scroll in all directions.

The good news: You can limit the usable dimensions of a page in advance, for example, to the size of the Letter format.

1. Open the **View** menu and select **Paper Size**.

2. A new task pane gets docked to the right, where you may fill in the desired page dimensions and orientation. The uppermost list lets you choose from various fixed standard sizes, such as "Letter". You may also define a custom page size.

3. In addition you may adjust the print margins for the page, just like in a word processor.

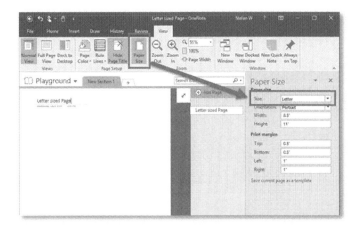

 Click **Save current page as a template** to reuse it whenever needed.

 You may also limit the dimensions of existing pages already filled with content, but, all elements located outside of the defined borders have to be moved manually to inside the valid area.

6 Removing empty space

The command description "Insert space" doesn't indicate that you can actually use this function to do the opposite as well - remove any empty space that may be the result of having deleted some content. To remove space you don't have to select all containers below the empty space and drag everything up using the mouse. Instead, just select **Insert – Insert Space** and move the mouse cursor into the note content.

The typical horizontal line is displayed at the cursor position. Now just move it to the bottom margin of the empty area you want to remove. Press the mouse button and drag the line upwards. All content that is located below the line will follow.

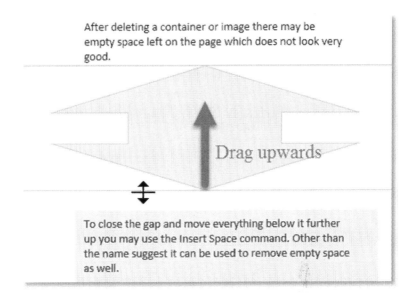

After deleting a container or image there may be empty space left on the page which does not look very good.

Drag upwards

To close the gap and move everything below it further up you may use the Insert Space command. Other than the name suggest it can be used to remove empty space as well.

Unfortunately this is limited to the horizontal dimension. You cannot close a vertical gap that way. The only method to move existing content to the left or right is to select everything (for example, by drawing a selection frame around them) and drag all objects using the mouse.

7 Forcing the creation of a new container

Sometimes you may want to create multiple containers right underneath each other, for example to make it easier to drag them to another location on the page later. You may find that it seems impossible to do: If you just click a few lines below an existing container, OneNote will simply add another couple of empty lines to it instead of creating a new one.

Still, creating multiple containers right below each other is very much possible. The trick is to double-click at the new position to create a new container. This also works right below an existing container.

8 Moving pages including subpages

OneNote allows page groups consisting of pages, sub-pages and sub-sub-pages. It's very easy to change the hierarchical level of any page: In the page tabs list, just click and drag a page title to the right or back to the left. OneNote will automatically change the indentation of the page accordingly.

But when moving or copying a page to another position in the page tab list or to another section or notebook, its indented sub-pages won't follow along (see picture below).

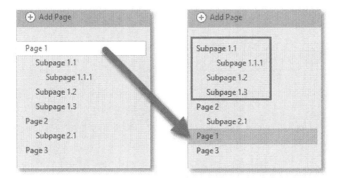

A workaround would be to manually select all the pages and sub-pages you want to move while keeping the **[Ctrl]**-key pressed – an error-prone and not very convenient method. There is a much better way:

1. First collapse all sub-pages. To do this, just click on the "^"-Symbol that appears to the right of the page title when you move the mouse cursor onto it. Now only the title of the top page is displayed. Indicators for existing but collapsed subpages are the stack display of the title frame and the permanent display of a "**v**"-symbol. Alternatively, press keyboard shortcut **[Ctrl] + [Shift] + [8]**. You can use this keyboard shortcut from any page within a page group.

2. Move the top page to the desired position. All sub-pages will follow. After moving you may expand the sub-page list again by clicking on the "**v**"-symbol.

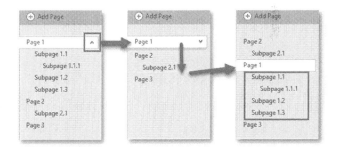

9 Moving PDF files including annotations

All containers, inserted files, pictures or other elements on a notebook page are separate entities. You cannot combine these objects into groups like you can in some graphics programs. This also applies to PDF printout images containing annotations you applied using the highlighter, drawing or handwriting tools. These annotations are, in fact, anchored to the page canvas not to the object right next to the annotation.

If you move an annotated object, all its annotations will stay in place and will therefore appear misaligned. As long as Microsoft does not implement a grouping function (see the note below), there is only one way to avoid this.

Before moving an object you have to select all other objects you want to move along with it. You can click and drag your mouse to create a selection frame, select individual objects using the **[Ctrl]**-key, or use keyboard shortcut **[Ctrl] + [A]**. This behavior is not limited to PDF printouts. It works for all other types of content, such as pictures or typed text with annotations, as well.

When this book was being written, Microsoft had just released an update for the Windows 10 App version of OneNote. This update includes an option to combine several graphic objects into one. But currently this functionality has not been implemented for One-Note 2016 and – more importantly – it does not solve the problem with annotated documents. The grouping option is limited to drawings, shapes and handwriting only – pictures and printouts (PDFs) still cannot be grouped with anything.

10 Locking the position of PDF documents

After inserting a file printout into OneNote, for example from a PDF document, you may want to prevent the printout image from accidentally being moved around.

This is possible by converting the printout image into a page background: Open the object's context menu by right-clicking it and selecting *Set Picture as Background*. This prevents any change of position and size. Note that this protects the picture only – everything on top of it (annotations, drawings, additional text) can still be moved.

If you want, you can bring the picture back to the page foreground by right-clicking on the page canvas and selecting the same *Set Picture as Background* option again.

You can also move text or any other object to the page background, but it requires a few extra steps:

1. Select these objects and cut them to the Windows clipboard with *Start – Cut* or keyboard shortcut **[Ctrl] + [X]**.

2. Paste the clipboard contents as a picture, using *Start – Paste – Picture*. You can also use keyboard shortcut **[Ctrl] + [V]**, **[Ctrl]**-key, **[U]**.

3. Right-click the image and select *Set Picture as Background* from the context menu.

Note that if you convert text, ink and other objects to images in this way, their original format cannot be restored. Imagine that you have converted a piece of text to an image and sent it to the page background. You can pull that image back from the background but it will remain an image. At best, you can retrieve the text from the image, but its original formatting is lost permanently.

A recently added option in OneNote 2013 and 2016 allows you to insert printouts (not images) as background by default. You just have to open the OneNote Settings and check *File – Options – Advanced – Printouts – Automatically set inserted file printouts in the background*.

11 Panning a page using the mouse

While you can easily pan a note page around using your finger on a Windows tablet, this does not work with your mouse on desktop computers – not even in conjunction with [Ctrl] or [Alt] as most graphic programs do.

Still there is a panning command in OneNote. It's called *Panning Hand*. It is somewhat hidden in the Tools command group on the *Draw* menu, and only visible if you are using a non-touch device. When activated, it changes the mouse pointer to a hand symbol and lets you move the page content around using the mouse. To disable panning mode, you would have to click it again or click on the *Type* command or press **[Esc]**.

Even with the Panning Hand command in the ribbon, it's not very convenient to find and activate every time you just want to shift your page around a bit. So let's make this command always available, regardless of the menu ribbon displayed.

1. You can add the Panning Hand command to the Quick Access Toolbar. One way to do this is *File – Options – Quick Access Toolbar*. Set the list to the left from *Popular Commands* to *All Commands*, select the *Panning Hand* command from the alphabetic command list and click on the *Add >>* button. You can now move the command to a specific position in the toolbar (maybe to the first/top one) by using the arrow buttons to the right. A much quicker way is to right-click on the ribbon command and select *Add to Quick Access Toolbar*, but unfortunately this is only possible on non-touch devices.

2. You can now switch the Panning Hand command on and off, depending on its position inside the toolbar, by using the keyboard shortcut **[Alt] + <position nr>**. For example, if you moved the command to the far left, the corresponding keyboard shortcut would be **[Alt] + [1]**.

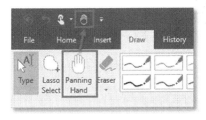

Now if your mouse is a configurable one, you may open its settings program and assign this shortcut to an unused mouse button (maybe the one under the mouse wheel). From now on you would just have to press that button to toggle the panning mode on and off.

12 Doing math in OneNote

Did you know that you can do simple mathematical calculations ("napkin math") directly in OneNote? This is how you do it:

Enter the math expression somewhere inside a text container directly followed by an equals sign (=).

Example: **1200*1.19=**

As soon as you hit **[Space]** or the **[Return]**-key, the answer is added behind the equals sign.

Example: **1200*1.19=1428**

You can combine multiple operations in one string.

Example: **(8-3)*7+65=**

By using the **[Return]**-key instead of the **[Space]**-key, the equation is resolved and a new line is created. In both cases the result will not replace the equation but is simply added behind the "=". If you just want the resulting value you would have to erase the equation manually.

 Don't include spaces in the expression. Just type numbers, operators and functions as a single, continuous string.

In addition to the operators **+-*X/%^!()** you may use the following functions:

ABS, ACOS, ASIN, ATAN, COS, DEG, LN, LOG, LOG2, LOG10, MOD, PI, PHI, PMT, RAD, SIN, SQRT and **TAN**. All functions may be written in upper or lower case.

You can disable this feature in the OneNote settings: Select *Start—Options—Advanced*. Under *Editing*, remove the check mark at the option *Calculate mathematical expressions automatically*.

There is also an equation editor for entering (but not solving) more complex formulas. You find it under *Insert – Equation*. You may use the syntax from LaTex also used on Wolfram Alpha to enter formulas or even use your pen to draw them (*Draw – Ink to Math*).

In OneNote 2013 you can also add Microsoft's free Mathematics Add-In for Office. At the time this book was being printed, the Add-In won't work for One-Note 2016.

13 Coloring a text container

OneNote doesn't offer an option to colorize the background of a whole text container. Yes, you may always define the background color of selected text, but then only the characters themselves are colorized. The rest of the container will keep the page background color, usually White.

There's a trick to get the desired effect using the option to colorize table cells. To do so you put the text inside a table that contains just a single cell. Then you may choose a background color for that cell by selecting **Table Tools – Layout – Shading**. This command is also available via the context menu (right-click, **Table - Shading**).

Left and right borders may be applied by adding empty colorized columns. To add an additional border above and below the text you may insert empty lines (not paragraphs) with **[Ctrl]** + **[Return]**. Finally remove the cell borders with **Table Tools – Layout – Hide Borders**.

Note that the option to colorize table cells has been added with OneNote 2013. So you cannot use this method with a prior version, such as OneNote 2010.

14 Adding a (colorized) border around an image or text

When you insert an image into OneNote, it may come in handy to quickly put a border around the image. Adding a border is particularly useful if the image has a lot of white areas along the edges, making it less clear where the image ends and the background begins. With texts, borders add more weight and improve the visibility of your text, especially against a colorized page background. Borders can be simply black or colorized. Example of a text with a colorized border:

> Lorem ipsum dolor sit amet, consectetuer adipiscing elit. Maecenas porttitor congue massa. Fusce posuere, magna sed **pulvinar** ultricies, purus lectus malesuada libero, sit amet commodo magna eros quis urna.

This tip uses the fact that you can put images and text inside a OneNote table cell. The cell borders automatically become the borders of the image or text. To colorize the border, we use the cell Shading feature. This tip also illustrates how you can instantly insert an object into a new table.

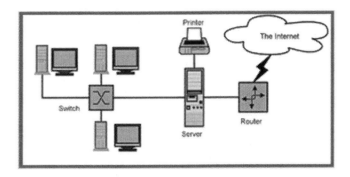

Adding a (colorized) border around an image

1. Click on the image to select it.

2. Insert a one-cell table by opening the **Table** command from the **Insert** menu tab and selecting a 1x1 table. This automatically places the image in that one-cell table and causes a border to appear around the image.

3. Because the table still has cursor focus, a special ribbon menu is available, called **Table Tools**. Open **Table Tools – Layout – Shading** and select the desired color for the border.

Adding a border around text

1. Select the text with your mouse or use **[Ctrl] + [A]**.

2. Insert a one-cell table by opening the **Table** command from the **Insert** menu tab and selecting a 1x1 table. This automatically places the text in that one-cell table and causes a border to appear around the text.

3. While the entire table is still selected, repeat step 2. The text now has a double border around it. The whole object remains selected for the next step.

4. From the **Table Tools** menu tab, select **Layout – Shading** and pick the desired color for the outer border. Both tables are now colorized in that same color.

5. Click in the inner table and repeat step 4. Make sure to pick the color White in the top-left corner of the color picker if you want a white background for your text. A white background is especially helpful when the text is positioned against a colorized page background.

15 Table inside a table inside a table...

Did you know that you can place a table inside a table cell? Even multiple nests are allowed, so you can have a table inside the cell of a table that is inside the cell of a table. To do this you just have to place the cursor in a table cell and then select *Insert – Table*. The height of the cells in the same row is automatically adjusted. You cannot manipulate cell height directly, only by entering content that takes up vertical space.

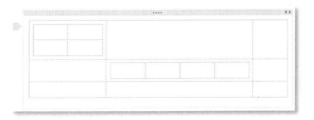

What is it good for? In OneNote, tables are mostly used to design and structure content. Nesting tables gives you more flexibility to do that. Try colorizing cell backgrounds, hiding table borders and inserting images into table cells.

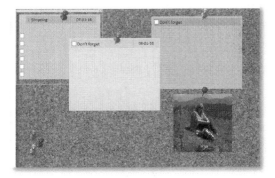

The Post-it™-Notes above are nothing more than 1-cell tables containing another table (one row, two columns) for the headline and date. Corkboard and pins are just background graphics.

16 AutoCorrect phrase expansion

Maybe you already know the AutoCorrect function from Word. AutoCorrect can be used to fix common typing mistakes as well as to enter recurring phrases by just entering a short abbreviation like "br" for "best regards". You may also want to use the auto-correction feature for recurring names, URLs and mail addresses. The same AutoCorrect mechanism is also available in OneNote. Here's how to use it:

1. Select *File – Options – Proofing*.

2. Click on the *AutoCorrect Options* button.

3. The following dialog box lets you set some standard proofing options such as correcting two capital letters at the beginning of a word. Below that you find a table containing common mistakes or abbreviations in the left column. They are automatically replaced by the ex-pressions or word in the right column. To create a new entry, you just have to enter a word or shortcut into the *Replace:* field and its replacement into the *With:* field.

4. To save the new entry, click on the *Add* button.

Now you just have to type the abbreviation, followed by a space or return. It will be replaced by the assigned expression.

If you are using auto correction for exchanging abbre-viations or shortcuts with words or phrases here is a suggestion: add a leading special character to the shortcuts, for example a hashtag (#). That way you may still use the abbreviation in a text without having it autocorrected.

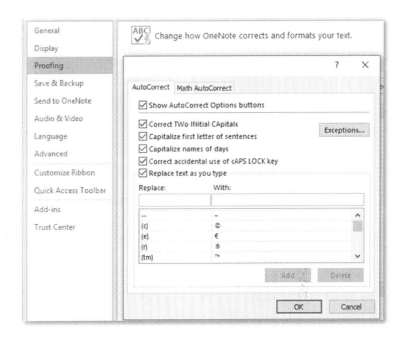

Apart from expanding abbreviations into full sentences, a good use for AutoCorrect is to have it insert a frequently used symbol that is missing from your keyboard. For example: The long em-dash, which is used to break up a sentence to denote a side thought, could use three single dashes --- and have these automatically replaced by a long em-dash —.

The list of auto-correction phrases is stored on your local PC in a file shared with other programs from the MS Office suite. So all entries you may add or change in OneNote are available in Word also and vice versa. The auto-correction feature is still available if you are using the free version of OneNote 2016 and Word or MS Office is not installed.

17 Restoring image and printout sizes

When larger images or printouts are inserted or pasted into a OneNote page, they are usually being scaled to smaller dimensions by OneNote automatically. While this is useful in most cases, sometimes you just want the original size.

First: Don't worry. The original resolution and quality are preserved (as well as the amount of storage space needed). OneNote is just displaying the image at a smaller size.

This behavior cannot be changed. But you may restore the display size of selected images to their original dimensions:

> - Right-click the image or printout to open the context menu.
> - Select the command **Restore to Original Size**.

If the command **Restore to Original size** is greyed out, then the image is already displayed with its original dimensions.

> When exporting an image from a note (right-click, **Save As...**) it is saved with its original resolution and dimensions. The original graphics format is also preserved. So JPG remains JPG, TIFF remains TIFF and so on.

18 Absolutely straight text highlighting

Have you ever tried to use the highlighters on the OneNote *Draw* menu with a mouse or a notebook touchpad? Most likely you found it impossible to draw anything even similar to a straight line. How about cheating a little bit:

- Select the marker of your choice from the *Draw* menu.

- On the *Shapes* gallery, click on the simple line or, better yet, a rectangle.

- Drag the line or rectangle over the text portion you want to highlight.

- If needed, adjust the position using the mouse while holding the **[Alt]**-key.

Now your highlights are as straight as if they were drawn with a ruler.

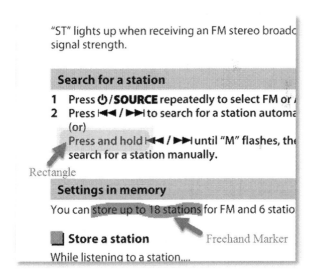

37

19 Additional OneNote windows

Navigating between pages can be a pain sometimes. For example, if you are working on one page and want to review something on another one, a lot of switching back and forth may be needed. Moving and copying bits of content between different pages or sections can be tedious too. You would always have to use the clipboard whereas simply dragging and dropping could be much faster.

So, why not open a second OneNote instance and place both windows side by side? Every window can show its own content, making navigating, researching and moving stuff around very easy. There are three straightforward ways to open another OneNote window:

- Press **[Ctrl]** + **[M]**

- Select *View – New Window*

- **[Shift]** + left-click on the OneNote icon in the Windows taskbar.

Windows 10 made it very easy to arrange windows on your screen by dividing it in halves or quarters. You may drag the windows to the left or right border of the screen or **[Shift]**+right-click on the taskbar icon, then select the *Show all windows side by side* from the context menu. You may also use the cursor keys while pressing and holding the **[Win]**-key.

20 Distraction-free editing and presenting

To let your thoughts flow freely, screen elements such as menus, section tabs, buttons and page lists may just be too distracting. In addition, they use up too much space on smaller screens. You can temporarily hide some of these UI elements, and its sometimes even better to just have a big empty sheet.

It's easy in OneNote: Just press **[F11]** to remove most UI elements and get an almost empty page to take notes on. Almost all UI elements? Correct. In the upper-right corner there is still an expandable list of notebooks and sections.

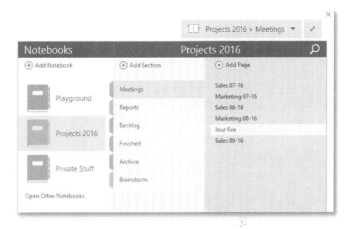

Quick Notes – the "Post-It™" style function available even when OneNote isn't running – is a way to get a note page that's even "more empty". Here's how you do it:

1. Create a new Quick Note: Press **[Win]** + **[N]** in OneNote 2016. OneNote 2013 needs you to press **[N]** again after releasing the **[Win]**-key or use **[Win]** + **[Alt]** + **[N]** instead.

2. This opens a new Quick Note, a small note sheet with a pink background, usually appearing somewhere in the middle of your screen.

3. If the pink background color bothers you, you can change it by clicking on the triple-dot title bar and selecting the desired background color (or none) from *View – Page Color*.

4. Now press **[Win]** + **[Cursor Up]**. This expands the note to fill up the whole screen area.

There is no notebook or section list shown now. Just a plain, blank space to write or draw on to to your heart's delight. The only remaining element is a small grey bar at the top with three dots in it. Clicking on that makes the ribbon and Quick Access Toolbar appear. Notebook and section navigation is still missing though, as the storage location for Quick Notes is fixed.

To hide the UI elements again you just have to click somewhere inside the note-taking area.

OneNote remembers the last size and position of the Quick Notes window. So pressing **[Win]** + **[Cursor Up]** is just needed the first time.

If you want to shrink the Quick Note window back to its default size just press **[Win]** + **[Cursor Down]**.

21 Entering symbols using Unicode values

Computer programs store individual characters as numeric values. In the early days of computing these were based on the ASCII character table. Nowadays, computer programs use a much larger table, called Unicode. In its current incarnation Unicode consists of 128,000+ characters, symbols and glyphs from many international writing scripts. The purpose of Unicode is to ensure a piece of text created in one computer program can easily be transferred to another program without the text getting garbled or mutilated. Each Unicode character has a 4-digit hexadecimal code value that refers to its position in the Unicode table, for example, 221E for the infinity symbol ∞.

OneNote offers a feature that lets you work directly with Unicode character values. If you know the numeric value of a Unicode character, you can manually enter it in OneNote. Conversely, OneNote can display the Unicode value of any character typed by anyone on a OneNote page. In both cases we use the keyboard shortcut **[Alt] + [X]**. Let's look at a few examples to see how this works.

If you know the Unicode value

In this case, you type the 4-digit hexadecimal value of the character, followed by **[Alt] + [X]**.

Example 1: 221E[Alt] + [X] to get the infinity symbol ∞. 221E is the Unicode value for the infinity symbol.

Example 2: 2013[Alt] + [X] to get the punctuation mark – (so-called *en-dash*). 2013 is the Unicode value for the en-dash.

If you want to know a character's Unicode value

In this case, you position the text cursor right behind a character and then press [Alt] + [X].

Example 1: ‰[Alt] + [X]
The character ‰ is replaced by **2030**, the Unicode value for *Per Mille Sign*.

Example 2: ♫ [Alt] + [X]
The character ♫ is replaced by **266B**, the Unicode value for *Beamed Eighth Notes*.

Exploring Unicode values

To find the Unicode value of a character from within OneNote, you can also use *Insert – Symbol – More Symbols*. For each font installed on your system, this dialog box lets you navigate the various Unicode subsets within that font (Basic Latin, Latin-1 Supplement, Latin Extended A etc.). Most fonts cover only specific Unicode subsets.

If you click on a character you can read its *Unicode name* and hexadecimal *Character code* at the bottom of the dialog box, just below the gallery of Recently Used symbols.

This same tip works in Word, Outlook and Power-Point. **[Alt] + [X]** doesn't work in Excel, but it does offer the *Symbol* dialog box from the *Insert* menu tab.

22 That pentagonal paragraph marker

In many ways the OneNote note editor works similarly to the one in Word. However, one clear distinction is how paragraphs are handled. A key instrument to work with paragraphs in OneNote is the solid-grey pentagonal paragraph marker that you see if you hover the mouse cursor over the left margin of a piece of text.

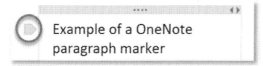

Example of a OneNote paragraph marker

Working with paragraph markers

As soon as you hover your mouse cursor over a OneNote paragraph marker, the mouse cursor changes into a four-arrowed cursor – an indication that you can manipulate that paragraph as a unit. Here are a couple of things you can do:

- Click the marker to select a single paragraph. You can also use the keyboard shortcut **[Ctrl]** + **[A]**.

- Select multiple paragraphs at a time by using **[Shift]**-Click (adjacent paragraph selection) or **[Ctrl]**-Click (non-adjacent paragraph selection).

- Click-and-drag paragraph markers to move their content to a different location within the same note container, or to drag them onto another note container. This also lets you smoothly change the order of items within bulleted or enumerated lists, or move rows up or down within a table.

- Click-and-drag paragraphs to the right or left to *Increase indent position* or *Decrease indent position*.

- Double-click a paragraph marker to collapse and expand any level in a multi-level outline. Collapsed levels are indicated by a + icon.

The paragraph marker context menu for text items

When you right-click on a paragraph marker, a context menu opens. This menu lets you Select all items of a multi-level outline that appear at the same outline level, for example, All at level 3.

To test this yourself, create a multi-level outline. Then:

1. Right-click on any pentagonal paragraph marker in front of any paragraph in the same note container.

2. Choose the *Select* command from the context menu, and then pick *All at level 3*.

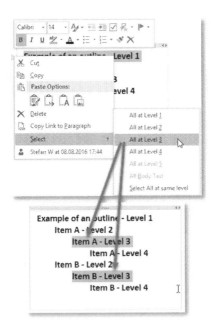

23 Splitting a table horizontally

To split a OneNote table into two separate tables, follow these steps:

1. Put the text cursor in the row after which you'd like to cut the table in two.

2. Press **[Ctrl]** + **[Enter]** to create a new table row.

3. Press **[Del]** to immediately delete the newly created row. This will cause a gap.

In general, pressing **[Del]** from the first cell in an empty row deletes that row. If you do that in the middle of a table, it creates a gap where that table row once was.

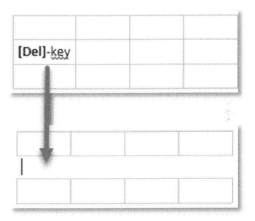

24 Keeping resized image proportions

When you select an image to resize it, you usually will want to retain the original width-to-height ratio.

If the image is <u>located inside a note container</u>, there is only one image selection handle that lets you do this; the one in the bottom-right corner.

Select your image and hover your mouse cursor over the bottom-right corner. You'll notice that the mouse cursor changes into a diagonal, double-arrowed cursor. You can now click-and-drag the mouse cursor inward or outward to resize the image with the original proportions remaining the same.

All other image selection handles have a different effect.

For images <u>located directly on the page canvas</u>, you can use the selection handles in any of the four corners of the image.

Chapter 2

Organize and Navigate

This section is all about organizing your notes and optimizing your work with OneNote.

25 Best notebook structures

...are a very individual matter. You may collect everything that you want to remember in one single OneNote notebook and rely on the search function. Or you may create a separate notebook for every project and subject. You may use as many sections as you want and group these sections in section groups. In turn, section groups can contain section groups of their own. Individual pages can have subpages at two levels. OneNote offers everything for those obsessed with orderliness, as well as for scatterbrains.

So it's totally up to you how you want to structure and organize your OneNote content. If you're not satisfied with one way of organizing, you can easily reconfigure everything by copying or moving around sections and pages at any time. In the desktop version of OneNote, you can even drag & drop items onto a different notebook in the notebook navigation list. But there are some things you might want to consider first.

Importance of search scope

The whole point of OneNote is not just storing lots of information, but more importantly, finding everything without needing to know the exact location of every bit of information.

The scope setting of the search feature allows you to narrow search results to just the current notebook or even the current section or page. However, only currently opened notebooks can be searched. Although the search scope menu has **All Notebooks** listed as an option, this actually refers to *open* notebooks only. The same is true for most versions of OneNote. At the moment, only OneNote for iPad and Mac are capable of searching notebooks not currently open inside the app. In OneNote Online search results are limited to the current section only.

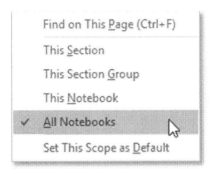

To reduce the number of notebooks currently open, consider creating only a few or even just a single notebook with multiple section groups.

 Please note that Section groups can only be moved, not copied. At least not without a certain amount of effort (manually create a group and copy sections).

Sharing notes

When you are sharing your notes with someone else, access is granted at the level of an entire notebook. This means you cannot share access to an individual page or section.

The only way to hide notes from prying eyes is by storing these notes in password-protected notebook sections. This process is somewhat cumbersome. Another issue is that you cannot search sections while they are locked. So if you only want to share very specific information with others, best practice is exactly counter to the previous advice: Instead of storing your notes in a limited number of notebooks, you'll need to create several notebooks - some for sharing and others for private use.

26 Stick to the left

This simple tip can save you a lot of inconvenience: If you want to access your notes on portable devices or smaller screens, it is best to insert your notes on the left-hand side of the page only. Avoid creating multiple text containers next to each other horizontally, as this will make it difficult to navigate your notes.

Scrolling horizontally is already tricky on a PC, let alone on a smartphone. To get a full view of your page, you'd have to zoom out up to the point where the text would become unreadable. So when feasible, keep your text and images to the left.

27 Moving a notebook to another location

Taking an entire OneNote notebook stored locally on a PC and moving it to Microsoft's cloud service OneDrive is easy.

Both OneNote 2013 and 2016 contain a feature that takes care of this automatically. You can find the option to move a notebook under *File – Share – Move Notebook*.

The process gets somewhat more complicated if the notebook is already stored with a cloud service, such as OneDrive, OneDrive for Business, or SharePoint Online. Do the following if you want to move a cloud-based OneNote notebook to another location in the cloud or to your local hard drive (the latter needs an Office-version of OneNote 2013/2016:

1. Open the existing notebook.

2. Create a new OneNote notebook at the desired destination, be it on your local hard drive (Office OneNote), OneDrive, OneDrive for Business or SharePoint. Just give your new notebook the same name as your old one, presuming no notebook with that same name exists yet.

3. Pin your notebook list to the side of your screen so that it always stays visible. To pin, click on the pin symbol in the top-right corner of the notebook list.

4. Fully expand both notebooks in the notebook list, so that all sections and section groups become visible.

5. Drag each of the sections and section groups one by one from the old notebook to the new notebook. If your old notebook was a shared notebook, it is best to leave one section with one note page behind. On this page you can leave a warning to indicate that the notebook has moved.

6. If your old notebook was shared with other people, you'll need to share the new notebook again for them to have access to it.

7. Lastly, close the old notebook.

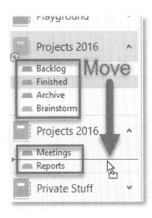 

28 Renaming a notebook (locally only)

If you don't like the name of your notebook anymore, you can change its display name. Note that the new name is only a cosmetic change applied locally. The original filename and notebook link will not be affected by the name change. This is to prevent shared notebooks from becoming inaccessible.

1. In the notebook list, point your mouse at the notebook you want to rename and right-click to open the context menu. Select **Properties...** from the context menu.

2. In the **Display Name** field of the Notebook Properties dialog box, enter the new name for the notebook.

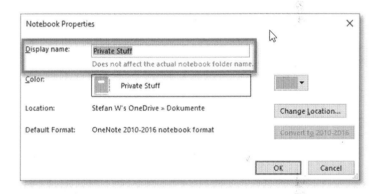

The new display name is only visible in the OneNote client in which you changed the name. Other users still see the original name. If they are using OneNote 2013 or 2016 they may change the name for themselves as well.

29 Deleting a notebook

Like most programs working with data files OneNote does not offer a command to delete a whole notebook from inside the program. How you get rid of an unwanted notebook depends on where it is stored. If you don't know it's location, open it in OneNote and click on **File**. You get a list of all currently opened notebooks with the storage path identified right below the names. Identify the notebook you want to delete and remember or copy its path.

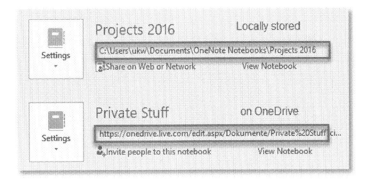

- Important: Close the notebook to be deleted.

- If the notebook is stored locally, use Windows Explorer to navigate to the corresponding path and delete the folder that is named like the notebook, which will include deleting all of its content.

- In the case of OneDrive or OneDrive for Business, the best method of deleting a notebook is by using your web browser. Navigate to **https://onedrive.live.com**. Find and select your notebook. It's shown just as a single link file instead of a folder. The actual notebook files are hidden; deleting the link will remove all hidden files. Delete by clicking on the trashcan symbol (**Delete** command). The link, the folder and the files will be gone.

30   Transferring custom tags

In addition to the default tags such as *To Do*, *Important* and *Question*, OneNote also offers a way to create custom tags. Each tag has a display name and, optionally, a symbol, a font color, a highlight color or a combination of these.

All OneNote clients, including the mobile versions, are capable of correctly displaying notes with custom tags. However, only OneNote 2013/2016 on a Windows PC lets you create or change custom tags. These custom tags are not stored in the notebook itself, but in a preferences file on the user's local profile. This is why custom tags don't appear in the Tags gallery on other computers in which you open the same notebook.

Microsoft does not offer an official method to transfer or copy custom tags from one PC onto another. Still, there's no need to manually redefine every single custom tag. You can add them back in using one of these two methods:

Method 1: On the PC missing the desired custom tags, open a OneNote page that already has another custom tag. Then, right-click on the tag symbol and select *Add to My Tags* from the context menu. Repeat this one by one for every different custom tag. To speed up this process, you may first create a note with all custom tags (on the PC which already has them in the tag list) applied to it and use this note to add the custom tags from.

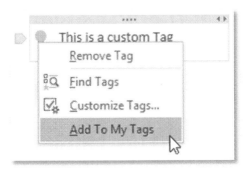

Method 2: The "Sledgehammer" method. OneNote stores custom tags in the file **Preferences.dat**, together with other settings such as the list of open notebooks. You can find this list at this file path:

C:\Users\<username>\AppData\Roaming\Microsoft\One-Note\<Version>.

Substitute *<Version>* with **15.0** for OneNote 2013 and **16.0** for OneNote 2016. First close OneNote on the destination PC, rename the original **preferences.dat** file to something else like **preferences.bak** (just in case and not to overwrite it) and then copy the new version to the same destination.

 With this method you will lose all settings contained in the preferences file on the destination PC.

31 Using multiple accounts

You may choose to use one or more additional Microsoft accounts. Maybe you want to separate business and private notes. Or you want to use the additional storage capacity of a second account.

Some OneNote clients (for example OneNote 2013/2016 for Windows) will allow you to login to more than one account at a time; some don't (like the Win 10 Universal app).

In any case there is a way to access notebooks on different accounts: Just share your notebooks on Account 2 with yourself (Account 1) granting full editing rights.

That way you only have to login to your main account on every OneNote client to be able to access and edit all notebooks on your additional accounts.

32 Copying sections using drag & drop

Moving sections from one notebook to another works seamlessly through drag & drop from the notebook navigation list pinned to the side of your screen. You can also drag & drop directly from the horizontal, colorized section tabs.

What about copying? That too is not a problem: Simply hold the **[Ctrl]**-key down while you drag a section to a new location. As soon as you let go of the mouse button, the section is copied. This even allows you to create a duplicate copy of a section inside the same notebook.

 Please note that this only works with sections, not with section groups.

33 Scrolling between pages in a section

Need to quickly browse through the pages in a section? There are two ways to do that.

- When the text cursor is somewhere on the current page, simply press [**Ctrl**] + [**PgDn**] or [**Ctrl**] + [**PgUp**] to quickly jump to the next or previous page in the current section.

- It's even faster if you have a mouse with a scroll wheel at your disposal. Hover your mouse pointer on the page navigation list, press the [**Ctrl**]-key and use the mouse wheel to scroll through the pages.

34 Sorting Pages

The sorting of pages listed in the page tabs list cannot be changed. Every time you add a new page, it is added to the bottom of the list by default. The order of existing pages can only be changed through drag & drop.

There is no built-in method in OneNote to sort pages by title, date or any other sort criterion. Still, there are two solutions that at least partly solve this problem by allowing you to sort existing pages. Newly created pages will be added at the bottom of the list again. So to sort the whole list you would have to repeat one of the following procedures.

Jan Roelof de Pijper's OneNote 2010 Sort Utility, originally published as part of a larger tools collection named *OneNote Powertoys*, also works fine with OneNote 2013/2016. You can find this tool at:

http://www.onenotepowertoys.com/2010/12/09/onenote-2010-sort-utility/

OneNote Sort Utility is not a OneNote add-in, but a separate Windows program. After you install and launch the program, a hierarchical tree of the currently opened notebooks is displayed. Expand one of the notebooks to mark the section or section group you want to order.

Next, determine whether the pages should be sorted by name or by date last modified. You can also select an ascending or descending sort. Finally, click the **Sort**-button.

OneNote Sort Utility can parse notebooks recursively, which means that it can process a OneNote section group including all the section groups, sections and pages contained within that notebook branch. Before executing the **Sort** command, the OneNote Sort Utility warns that the changes made by the program cannot be undone.

Your second option to sort pages is through the add-in **Onetastic** by Omer Atay (**https://getonetastic.com**), which offers a large library of tools and macros. After installing it you may download additional macros. One of these is for sorting OneNote pages.

35 Creating a page in the middle of the page list

As described in the previous tip, OneNote creates new pages at the bottom of the page tabs list by default. Although you cannot change this default behavior, you can still prevent it - albeit one page at a time. Simply point your mouse cursor to an existing page and press the right mouse button. This opens the context menu for that page. Now, select the *New Page* command. You may also use the keyboard shortcut **[Ctrl] + [Alt] + [N]**.

Even more elegant: Use your mouse. But first you have to make sure that a certain setting is activated:

1. Open the *File* menu and select *Options – Display*.

3. Put a checkmark in the option *Show the floating New Page button near page tabs*.

4. Save the settings with *OK*.

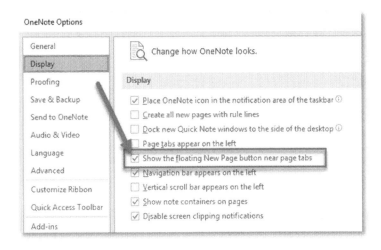

You'll notice a pentagon icon appearing in the margin of the page tab list, right where you point with your mouse. Clicking on that symbol inserts a new page at that position:

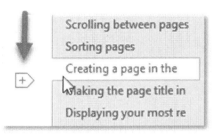

36 Making the page title invisible without removing it

If you prefer not to show the page title and creation date, you can easily hide them through *View – Hide Page Title*. OneNote will prompt you to confirm that the page title will be removed.

This approach does have a drawback - hiding the page title this way, in fact, deletes the page title entirely. Thereafter, the page tabs list will no longer show the original page title, but the first words from the page content. This means you'll need to edit the page content to make sure the page tab for this page contains useful information about the contents of your page.

Here's a suggestion: After hiding the page title, create a new text container in the top-left corner of the screen. Type your text in a text color that blends completely with the page background, e.g. white on a white page background color. Then set the font size to the minimum size of 6 pts.

Of course you could make the regular OneNote page title invisible in a similar fashion, saving you the hassle of adding a new text container. Unfortunately by working this way, you won't be able to hide the horizontal line in the page title. The only way to hide this horizontal line is by using the **Hide Page Title** command.

To edit your custom 'page title' do *not* use the **Rename** function from the page tab's context menu, as that would restore a regular, empty page title at the top of the page.
Instead, on the page you placed the hidden, custom 'page title' text container, point your mouse towards the top-left corner. As soon as the rectangular shape of the text container is displayed, you can double-click on the page title and edit it.

Save an empty page with a hidden page title as a OneNote page template. If you want, you can enable this page template to be active for all new pages created in the current section.

37 Displaying your most recent notes

Many times while working with OneNote, you'll want to quickly create a list of the notes you've been working on in the past few days. It could be that you just can't seem to remember what the notes were about, or in which notebook and section you stored them.

In Evernote the standard view is chronological. In OneNote for Windows 10, OneNote for Android, and iOS apps, there is an optional recent page view. Maybe this will come to the desktop version of OneNote in the future as well. Maybe.

There are two options that will give you at least a similar result in OneNote 2013/2016:

You can use the free tool OneCalendar. This program is installed as part of the Onetastic add-on for OneNote (**https:/getonetastic.com**), and you can also install it as a separate tool.

OneNote itself also offers an historical search feature. It's somewhat hidden:

1. Open the **History** menu.

2. In the ribbon group **Authors**, select **Recent Edits**.

3. A drop-down menu will open, showing several time frames – e.g. **Today** or **Last 7 Days**. Select one of these options. This will now function as a search query.

A search results task pane will open, listing all notes edited in the chosen timeframe. Click on a search result and the page will open instantly.

If you use the **Recent Edits** views more often, then consider adding a custom command for this to your Quick Access Toolbar or Ribbon. In the OneNote option sections **Customize Ribbon** and **Quick Access Toolbar**, first select **Choose Commands from – All Commands**. This opens an alphabetically ordered list of commands. Next, look for **Last 7 Days** under "L", or for **Today** under "T" and add either or all of these to your command bar.

38 Search syntax (AND / OR)

In most cases you will want to use a single word with OneNote's search feature. OneNote doesn't offer any advanced search syntax. This would even be difficult to accomplish as OneNote pages don't have structured elements.

Still, you can use multiple search words in your search query and combine them using AND, OR and quotation marks. For example:

apple juice - will find all pages containing both keywords in any order.

app ju - because OneNote searches incrementally, just typing a few letters of each word will find a match too. This is referred to as implicit truncation.

apple AND juice (note the all-uppercase spelling for "AND"!) - same result. In other words, AND has no additional effect.

apple OR juice - displays all pages containing just one or both keywords in any order.

"apple juice" (enclosed in quotation marks) - now the query is executed as a literal search. To show up in the search results, the spelling on a page needs to match the search query exactly. This is called a phrased search.

 Currently this search behavior only applies to the desktop versions of OneNote (OneNote for Windows and Mac, and OneNote App Store Version) and to OneNote for iOS. The other OneNote clients behave distinctly differently. It is likely that Microsoft will change and adapt this in the future.

39 Keep your notebooks open

Notebooks that you rarely or no longer use can be closed. Closing a notebook removes it from the list of notebooks. Do do that right-click the name of the notebook and select **Close This Notebook** from the context menu.

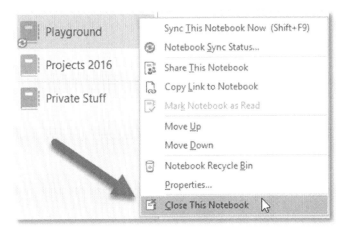

Advantages: The notebook list is less cluttered and you're saving some disk space, because closing a notebook also deletes the local cache files.

But this also means, that as soon as you open the notebook again, its entire contents will have to be reloaded from the notebook's cloud storage space. Especially when a notebook is stored on OneDrive, OneDrive for Business or SharePoint Online, this can take quite a long time.

Another disadvantage of closing a notebook is that you can no longer search for information stored in that notebook.

The conclusion is clear: If you need to use a notebook often, then keep it open at all times. To reduce the clutter, it usually suffices to collapse all notebooks in the notebook navigation list so that only their names are visible or unpin the notebook list.

40 Cleaning up a notebook before sharing

Before you share or publish a notebook, you may want to wipe edit traces, comments and personal notes from it. Here are some of the steps you could take to clean up your notebook:

From the *History* menu:

- select *Notebook Recycle Bin – Empty Recycle Bin*

- select *Notebook Recycle Bin – Disable History for This Notebook*

- select *Page Versions – Delete All Versions in Notebook*

- select *Page Versions – Disable History for This Notebook*

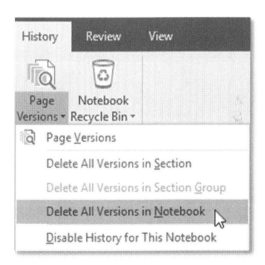

If you have Omer Atays Onetastic add-in installed, you may also download a macro that completely clears all Author references.

41 How much space are your notebooks occupying?

If you store your OneNote notebooks on your local hard drive or on a LAN drive, calculating how much space they occupy is easy. In Windows File Explorer, simply expand the subfolder where your notebook is stored and the file sizes of the notebook sections are listed together with the notebook name. As every notebook uses a folder of its own, you can also right-click on a notebook folder and consult the *Properties* to get the size occupied by that notebook.

If you store your notebooks on OneDrive, it's not possible to use the same method. Even though File Explorer displays the notebook names stored in OneDrive in the local sync folder of your PC, these are only placeholder links of around 1 KB.

It's good to understand that the OneDrive storage allowance provided to you by Microsoft is considerable, but not unlimited. How much space you have depends on your license, and on any complimentary bonus upgrades you may have earned in the past. You can check how much storage space you have and how much of that space has already been used up by OneNote notebooks. To see your storage allowance and how much of that is already used, visit **http://onedrive.live.com** and focus on the bottom-left corner of the browser window:

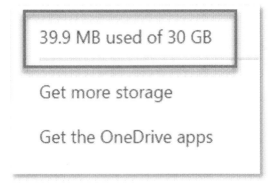

39.9 MB used of 30 GB

Get more storage

Get the OneDrive apps

If you have a lot of files, it may take a while before the entire page has completed and the amount of storage space is displayed. The displayed amount is a hyperlink. To see more details about your storage plan, click on the hyperlink.

To find out how large your OneNote notebooks are, navigate to the OneDrive folder where they are stored and switch the display from tiles to list. You will see how much space each notebook occupies in the right-most column:

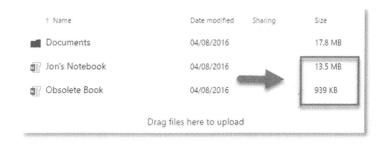

Unfortunately, there is no way to have these numbers added up by now. You have do this yourself to get an estimate of the total space occupied by your notebooks.

 With every notebook you create or open, OneNote also needs space to store the search index and cache files. The amounts for these files are only significant for your local storage space and do not get subtracted from your OneDrive allowance.

42 Moving pages conveniently

With OneNote it's easy to collect information and organize it later. OneNote even has a special collection bin for this, called the Quick Notes section. This catchall section is typically a receptacle for things such as short scribbles, web clippings, file printouts, document scans and content you forward by email.

When you're ready to organize your notes, there are two ways to move note pages to another location:

- Select one or more pages in the page tab list and right-click. You can also right-click on a notebook section. From the context menu, select the **Move or Copy** command. In the next dialog box, select the destination notebook / section and confirm by clicking on the **Move** or **Copy** button. You can also use the keyboard shortcut **[Ctrl] + [Alt] + [M]**. Note that OneNote lets you move a section group, but not copy it.

- Pin the notebook navigation list on the left side of the screen. With a swift movement, drag and drop your selected pages to the desired destination. No need to expand the destination notebook first - while dragging, the destination notebook will automatically expand. To copy pages with this method, keep the **[Ctrl]**-key pressed down.

Both of these methods work, but are a bit tedious. The first method involves quite a few clicks. With the drag-and-drop method it's easy to make a mistake: Your mouse button needs to stay pressed over a relatively long distance - from the page tab list on the right to the notebook navigation list on the left.

The following two suggestions improve the drag-and-drop method by significantly shortening the traveling distance of the mouse cursor. They also make it easier to move multiple pages to different targets.

Method 1: Dock the page tab list on the left side

The easiest way to shorten the mouse cursor's traveling distance is by displaying the OneNote page tab list on the left side. This will position the page tab list to the immediate right of the notebook navigation list. Here's how to enable that option:

1. Select *File – Options – Display*

2. Click to check the option *Page tabs appear on the left*. When you're done organizing your notes, you can come back to this setting and disable it again.

3. Click the **OK** button to confirm your settings.

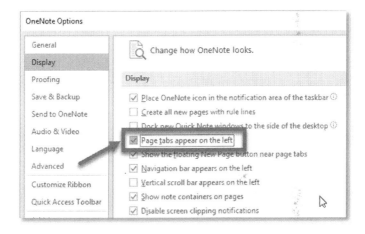

 This method has a tiny drawback. Your drag-and-drop move needs to be swift and short. If you hover the mouse cursor for longer than a second over the target section in the page navigation list, that section will expand and the current page (or the one you are pointing at) will be displayed in the OneNote editor. This is inconvenient because you'll need to manually navigate back to the page you were editing before.

Method 2: Two OneNote windows side by side

This method takes advantage of the fact that you can open several instances (windows) of OneNote 2013/2016 and the window-docking abilities of Windows – starting with version 7 and greatly improved in Windows 10.

1. Open a second OneNote instance with the keyboard shortcut **[Ctrl] + [M]**.

2. Point your mouse cursor to the OneNote icon on the Windows taskbar and Shift + right-click. Select *Show all windows side by side* from the context menu.

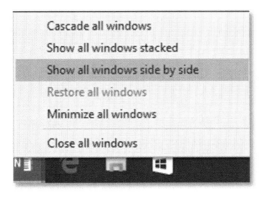

An alternative approach for step 2 is to use the Windows Snap feature: Click on the first OneNote instance and press **[Win] + [Cursor Left]**. This will cause that window to snap to the left side of the screen. Next activate the second OneNote instance and press **[Win] + [Cursor Right]**.

Both instances of OneNote are now snapped side by side. In the OneNote instance displayed on the right-hand side, anchor your notebook navigation list by clicking on the pin icon at the top of the list.

The page tab list of the left window is now positioned beside the notebook navigation list of the right window. This makes dragging and dropping much easier.

Snapping multiple OneNote instances in this manner is different from docking a OneNote page using the *View – Dock to Desktop* command. If you dock a OneNote page, both the page tab list and the notebook navigation list are hidden. This makes the Dock to Desktop feature unsuitable for organizing your notes.

The Snap Assist feature of Windows 10 makes selecting and snapping application windows even more flexible. After the first window has been snapped, Windows will list an overview of the remaining application windows in the other half of the screen, letting you pick the application window for the other half of the screen. By using the **[Win]** + **[Cursor Up]** and **[Win]** + **[Cursor Down]** key, you can even snap 2x2 windows in this manner.

43 Speed up the loading process

Ok, the title of this tip is not exactly correct. You cannot speed up the loading time when opening a Notebook. Especially when the notes are stored on OneDrive and the notebook is really big, this process may take quite a while. That's why we usually advise keeping frequently used notebooks open. Closing them causes the local cache files to be erased. The next time you need specific information from that notebook you would have to open it, which always means a complete download.

While the download is in progress, you cannot even use the search function. Well you can, but it would only search those sections and pages that have already been transferred. The ones still missing are not searched at all. You can easily identify those: The section tabs not downloaded yet are grey colored.

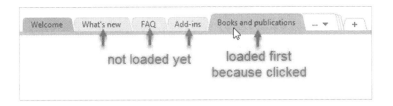

But instead of waiting until all notebook content is downloaded, you can change the order of the download. If you happen to know in what section the information you are looking for is stored, just click on its tab – even if it's still grey. OneNote will pause the ordered section-by-section download and immediately proceed with the section you have clicked on.

Thus you may have to wait only a few seconds before you can browse or search that section while the rest of the notebook will continue downloading.

44 In-page TOC with Paragraph Links

On a page with multiple paragraphs, it can be useful to have a table of contents (TOC) at the start of the page. Each item in the TOC will point to the corresponding paragraph. Here's how you can create such a TOC really quickly:

1. Select all paragraphs that you want to reference from the TOC.

2. Right-click and select **Copy Link to Paragraph** from the context menu.

3. Go to the top of the page using **[Ctrl]+[Home]**.

4. Press Enter a few times, and Paste with **[Ctrl]+[V]**.

OneNote Paragraph Links can also point to text outlines, images and table cells.

Pages with paragraph links are powerful but fragile: If you move pages with paragraph links to another notebook, the links will be broken.

45 Turning paragraphs into pages

OneNote offers a very useful feature that lets you instantly turn a list of items into individual pages.To explain how this feature works, let's start off with a simple task list for an upcoming trip, where each task needs to be assigned a separate page in the current notebook section:

Book flight
Plan itinerary
Make hotel reservations
Sightseeing research
Packing list

Select this list so that the five items become highlighted, right-click the list, and select *Link to Pages* from the context menu.

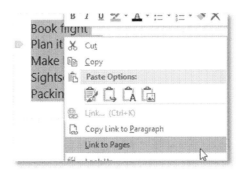

OneNote will instantly create five new, empty pages in the current section. Each page will have the item's content as its page title. At the same time, the list items have been converted to internal links, pointing to the corresponding pages.

Note that the *Link to Pages* feature only appears on the context menu of lists that consist of at least two elements.

46   Removing notebooks shared with you

Being able to share notebooks and other files through OneDrive.com and OneDrive for Business is great, but there's also a downside: After a while all those notebooks shared with you can really pile up. Here's how you can remove yourself from notebooks you once were granted access rights to:

Removing yourself from notebooks on OneDrive

1. In OneNote 2013/2016, close the shared OneNote notebooks you no longer need access to. To do this, right-click on the notebook name and select **Close This Notebook** from the context menu.

2. Sign in to **http://onedrive.live.com** with your Microsoft ID.

3. From the menu on the left, select **Shared**. You will now see different groups for files that you have shared with others and files that others have shared with you.

4. To select files, hover your mouse cursor on the top-right corner of a file icon. A circle icon will appear that you can click to select the file. You can select multiple files at a time.

5. When done selecting files, right-click and select **Remove from shared list** from the menu. The same option appears in the ribbon at the top of the screen.

6. A dialog box appears to confirm the removal. If you are sure that you no longer want access to these files, click **Remove**.

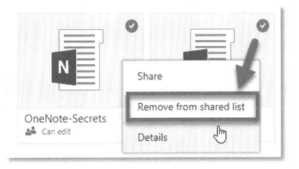

Removing yourself from notebooks on OneDrive for Business

1. In OneNote 2013/2016, close the OneNote notebooks you no longer need access to. To do this, right-click on the notebook name and select **Close This Notebook** from the context menu.

2. Sign in to **http://office.com** with your Office 365 credentials.

3. Open the OneDrive for Business app.

4. From the menu on the left, select **Shared With Me**. If so desired, use the **Sort** button in the top-right corner.

5. To select files, hover your mouse cursor to the left of a file icon. A circle icon will appear that you can click to select the file. You can select multiple files at a time.

6. When done selecting files, click on the option **Remove from shared list** that appears in the ribbon at the top of the screen.

7. A dialog box appears to confirm the removal. If you are sure that you no longer want access to these files, click **Remove**.

47 Prepare content for better retrieval

The essential part of using OneNote effectively is to be able to find information. There are a couple of best practices to make that easier.

Include synonyms and alternate spellings

Unlike web search engines, OneNote can only find words if they are literally included on the page. This means that by adding synonyms, alternate spellings and related words, you can improve the likelihood that that page will show up in OneNote search results.

For example, if your page is about OneNote in Education, then you may want to include 'teaching', 'students', 'learning', 'teachers', classroom', 'school'. This way the page can be found even if one of these alternate words is searched for.

OneNote search results order

When you perform a search in OneNote, search results are ordered by relevance:

- Recent picks - matching with most recently visited pages
- In title - match found based on the title: notebook title (most recently edited notebook first), section group title, section title, page title
- On page - match found in page body
- Deleted notes - match found in deleted page

What this means: Pay attention to choosing your page title carefully. Anything you put in the page title shows up first in the search results, so your page title should contain the most relevant words.

Page tabs list

If you're creating multiple pages with the same or almost the same words in the title, then make sure that at least the first few words of every page title are significant and distinctive. This helps to make the differences more obvious in the narrow page tabs list column.

48 Filtering Tag Summary Pages

Once you've tagged a number of items in your OneNote pages, you'll want to use the *Find Tags* feature to get an overview of your tags. This will open a task pane called *Tags Summary*. From here, you can click on the button *Create Summary Page*.

By default, the newly created Tag Summary Page will contain all tags listed on the Tags Summary task pane. There may be times when you only want a summary page showing specific tags, or even just a single one. With the following trick you can filter which tags are actually sent to the Summary Page and which ones are suppressed.

Collapsing and expanding task pane group headings

When you open the Tags Summary task pane, all group headings are automatically displayed in *expanded* mode. You can collapse a group heading by clicking on the tiny triangle displayed to the right of each heading.

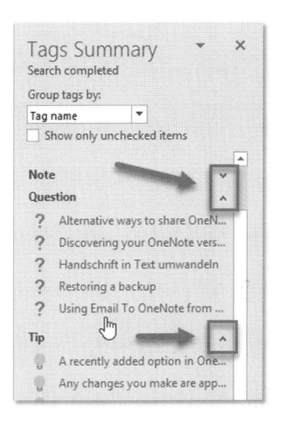

The important thing to know about collapsing a group heading is that it also causes all items under that heading to be suppressed in the Summary Page you generate based on these tags. In other words: Only tags from headings that are expanded in the Tags Summary task pane are, in fact, sent to the Tag Summary Page.

Chapter 3   Customize OneNote

If OneNote is to be integrated into your personal workflow - and that is ultimately the purpose of the program after all - it also needs to adapt to your personal habits and methods of working. This can be accomplished in certain areas. This chapter will show you a few rather hidden options for tweaking OneNote.

49   Repositioning the notebook bar and page tabs lists

By default, OneNote pins the expanded version of the notebook navigation bar to the left side of the screen. The page tabs list is located on the right. Both hese can be shifted to the opposite side:

- Open *File – Options – Display*.

- To pin the notebook navigation list to the right side, re-move the check mark from the option *Navigation bar appears on the left*.

- In the same options panel, you can enable the page tabs list to be displayed on the left by marking the option *Page tabs appear on the left*.

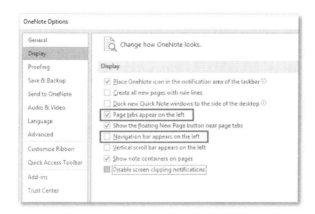

When the notebook navigation pane is in its collapsed state (unpinned), it will always appear on the left side of the screen. To display the list on the right, you need to pin it using the pin button in the top right corner of the notebook navigation pane.

If you display both the notebook navigation pane and the page tabs list on the same side, the notebook navigation pane will always appear on the far end.

50 Turning off the Mini Toolbar

In addition to the command ribbon and the Quick Access Toolbar, OneNote includes a third hovering toolbar called Mini Toolbar.

This toolbar appears when you select a piece of text and hover your mouse cursor over the selected text. The Mini Toolbar also pops up when you right-click a piece of text. The toolbar then appears together with a context menu.

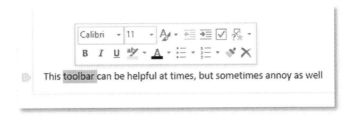

In some cases, the Mini Toolbar may be annoying, for example when it obscures some other important part of your screen. No worries, you can stop the Mini Toolbar from popping up at all.

- Open *File – Options – General*.

- Under User Interface Options, unselect the option *Show Mini Toolbar on selection*.

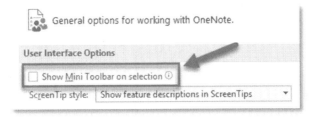

51 | The Quick Access Toolbar (QAT)

The Office ribbon interface has one drawback: Once you select a menu tab, the commands on all other menus are hidden. That's why all Office programs contain another customizable toolbar with button commands for frequently used commands, called the **Quick Access Toolbar** – aka **QAT**. By default, the Quick Access Toolbar is displayed in the top-left corner of the screen, just above the File menu tab.

The Quick Access Toolbar is a genius little helper that unfortunately gets easily overlooked. Its key advantage is that it's always in sight, no matter which menu tab on the ribbon is selected. It's also displayed when the ribbon is collapsed. The Quick Access Toolbar provides easy and quick access to the commands you use most often.

Adding and removing commands

By default, the Quick Access Toolbar contains just four commands:

- *Previous* (= go back to previously visited page)

- *Undo*

- *Dock OneNote to the desktop*

- *Customize Quick Access Toolbar*

If you click on the right-most command button of the Quick Access Toolbar, a drop-down menu will open with 12 suggestions for additional frequently used commands. For full customization control, including all commands that can be added to the Quick Access Toolbar, select *More Commands*. Alternatively, open these settings directly through *File – Options – Quick Access Toolbar*.

In the resulting dialog box you see two lists. By default, only the most frequently used commands are shown. To list all commands, open the drop-down menu labeled *Choose commands from* and select *All Commands*. You will now see all commands provided by OneNote itself and those provided by any add-ins you may have installed, ordered alphabetically by command name. The nice thing about this panel is that you will stumble across commands that are not available on any of the menu tabs on the ribbon. By clicking the *Add*-button, you can quickly add command buttons to the Quick Access Toolbar. You may change the order of the commands using the *Move Up* and *Move Down* buttons on the right-hand side of the panel. In a similar fashion, you can use the *Remove*-button to remove commands from the Quick Access Toolbar. When you're done, click the *OK* button.

Adding and removing commands - quick method

To quickly add a command from one of the menu tabs to the Quick Access Toolbar, locate the command on the ribbon and right-click its icon. Then select *Add to Quick Access Toolbar*. The command you selected will be added to the end of the Quick Access Toolbar. Similarly, you can right-click any command already on the Quick Access Toolbar and select **Remove from Quick Access Toolbar**.

Keyboard shortcuts

Commands on the Quick Access Toolbar can be accessed with a mouse click, but also through the keyboard by pressing [Alt] with a number key. More on this in the "Custom keyboard shortcuts" tip in Chapter 6.

Positioning the QAT under the ribbon

If you like, you can position the Quick Access Toolbar closer to the editing area, making it easier to reach the commands with your mouse cursor:

1. Click on **Quick Access Toolbar – Customize Quick Access Toolbar**.

2. From the drop-down menu, select the bottom command **Show Below the Ribbon**.

Of course you can always position the Quick Access Toolbar at the top of the screen again by selecting **Show Above the Ribbon**.

Smart commands to add to the QAT

The Quick Access Toolbar is particularly useful for commands that meet these criteria:

- Frequently used
- Not, or not easily, accessible through the ribbon
- No keyboard shortcut available.

Print and **Print Preview**
If you frequently need to print or print preview a OneNote page, the current, somewhat cumbersome, method requires you to open the *File* menu. From there you can select the *Print* option, and then select either *Print* or *Print Preview*. A much more convenient way is to add these commands to the Quick Access Toolbar. Note that the Print feature itself has a keyboard shortcut of its own - **[Ctrl] + [P]**.

Favorite pens and markers for drawing and handwriting
You can add as many as 8 *Favorite Pens* and 4 *Favorite Highlighters* to the Quick Access Toolbar. This is great for people with a stylus-enabled Windows tablet device, making OneNote's digital ink features instantly accessible. To complete the command set, add the button for your favorite type of *Eraser*.

Working off-line
OneNote synchronizes page updates automatically when an internet connection is available. If you want to disable synchronization, you can do so by right-clicking on a notebook name and choosing the *Notebook Sync Status* option from the context menu and then selecting *Sync manually*. If you use this feature often, it's much faster to add the *Work Offline* command to the Quick Access Toolbar.

Synchronization commands
When added to the Quick Access Toolbar, the *Sync* menu icon immediately changes when any of your notebooks has a synchronization issue. Likewise, the *Notebook Sync Status* command icon indicates whether the current notebook has a synchronization issue.

Always create pages with rule lines (or grids)
The option to always create pages with rule lines is located in *File – Options – Display*. There you can set the option *Create all new pages with rule lines*.

If you frequently work with pages with background rule lines or grids, you can instantly switch this option on and off right from the Quick Access Toolbar. Simply add the command **_Always cre-ate pages with rule lines_**. OneNote remembers the line type you selected last. Note that this setting also works for page grids.

Delete page

Deleting a page can be a bit of a hassle if you need to do this often. There is no ribbon command for it and no default keyboard shortcut. The official method is to right-click on a page tab in the page tabs list and then select **_Delete_** from the context menu. A much quicker method is to add the **_Delete Page_** command to the Quick Access Toolbar.

Resetting the Quick Access Toolbar

If, for some reason, you need to restore the original Quick Access Toolbar, you can do so with these steps:

1. Open File – Options – Quick Access Toolbar.Just above the OK button, locate the Reset button. Click this button to open the pull-down menu.

5. Select Reset Only Quick Access Toolbar.

6. Confirm the warning in the Reset Customizations dialog box.

7. Press the OK button.

52 Adding command groups to the QAT

Apart from individual commands, you can also add multi-function commands with submenus or galleries and even entire ribbon command groups to the Quick Access Toolbar. Additionally, you can define new, custom ribbon command groups from scratch and add those to the Quick Access Toolbar.

Adding submenus and galleries

When *All Commands* is selected in *File – Options – Quick Access Toolbar*, several commands appear with a tiny triangle on the right. These are commands that open a submenu or a so-called gallery. An example of a command with a submenu is *Review – Language.* Many other commands are galleries, for example the *Font* gallery on the *Home* menu, or the *Ink Styles* gallery on the *Draw* menu. Both of these multi-function command types can be added either through the dialog box in *File – Options – Quick Access Toolbar* or by right-clicking on a ribbon command and selecting *Add to Quick Access Toolbar*.

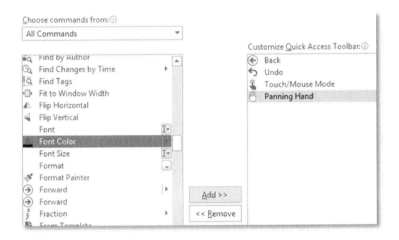

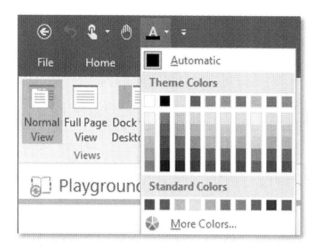

Adding entire command groups

At an even broader level, you can add entire command groups to the Quick Access Toolbar, straight from the ribbon. Let's assume you want to have the *Home – Basic Text* command group always available to you, no matter which menu tab is selected. Simply right-click in the bottom area of this command group just below the icons and select *Add to Quick Access Toolbar* from the context menu.

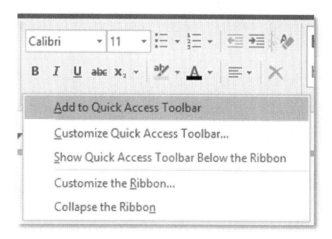

Adding custom ribbon command groups

In addition to adding entire ribbon command groups, you can also take a completely custom-defined ribbon command group and add that to the Quick Access Toolbar. This is a very powerful feature that allows you to combine frequently used commands into a group on the Quick Access Toolbar. Here's how to do this:

1. Open *File – Options – Customize Ribbon* and click on the *New Group* button. This will add a new group to an existing menu tab. Of course you can also create an entirely new menu tab first using the *New Tab* button and then add a *New Group* to the new menu tab.

2. Click on the *Rename* button to rename the new group and select a group icon. Assigning a group icon is important because it is this group icon that will be added on the Quick Access Toolbar.

3. Use the *Add* button to add any commands to your new group.

4. Save the settings by clicking on the *OK* button.

5. Back in the regular OneNote editing window, open the menu tab your new group is located in.

6. Right-click at the bottom of your new group and select *Add to Quick Access Toolbar* from the context menu.

53   Customizing the ribbon

If you find that the ribbon is too cluttered or that it contains commands you don't actually use, you can fully customize it. You may move commands around, remove them altogether or create new menu tabs with custom-defined command groups. To change the ribbon settings, visit *File – Options – Customize Ribbon*.

The *Customize Ribbon* dialog box behaves very similarly to the one for the Quick Access Toolbar. After you select *All Commands*, you will see all available commands in the column on the left.

There is one important difference between the Ribbon and the Quick Access Toolbar: Unlike the Quick Access Toolbar, which has a flat, non-hierarchical layout, the ribbon is *hierarchical*. Each menu tab consists of groups and commands. This hierarchical ribbon layout is reflected in the column on the right.

It is also important to know that ribbon commands can only be added to a *newly created* ribbon group. You cannot add a command to an existing ribbon group. Select an existing menu tab or create a *New Tab* and rename it as you like. Then create a *New Group* and rename it as well. Using the *Add* and *Remove* buttons located in between the two columns, you can now add commands to, and remove them from, the new group.

Unlike the Quick Access Toolbar, the *Customize Ribbon* dialog box contains an additional drop-down menu just above the right column. This drop-down menu contains an overview of the *Main Tabs*, and also of all *Tool Tabs* – the menu tabs that appear for specific operations. A good example of this is the *Table Tools* menu.

54 Setting the default font

OneNote offers various predefined text styles, e.g. *Heading 1..6*, *Citation*, or *Code*. Unlike Word, these styles cannot be customized. Nor can a new text style be added.

The only exception to the rigidity of these predefined styles is that the default font, designated as *Normal* in the text styles selection box, *can* be changed by the user. Upon OneNote installation, this font is set to Calibri 11pt. You can change the font name and font size as follows:

1. Go to *File – Options – General*.

2. Under *Default font*, you can adjust the font name, the font size and the font color.

3. Click on the *OK* button.

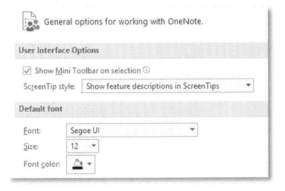

 Note that this setting affects OneNote 2013/2016 only. It has no effect on the font used in the mobile apps nor in the OneNote App for Windows 10.

55 Exporting and transferring menu settings

After manually tweaking your ribbon menus or Quick Access Toolbar, it would be nice if you could transfer these modifications to another computer without going through the same steps manually again.

All customizations to the ribbon and to the Quick Access Toolbar can be exported and then quite easily transferred to another computer also running OneNote 2013/2016. This process is the same no matter whether you use a perpetual Office license, the Office 365 subscription version or the free download of One-Note 2016. Here are the steps:

1. Open *File – Options – Customize Ribbon*.

2. Click on the button *Import/Export* and select *Export all customizations* from the drop-down menu.

3. In the resulting Explorer window, navigate to the desired file folder and adjust the file name "OneNote Customizations" as you see fit and click on the *Save* button.

On the target computer, follow step 1. In step 2, select *Import Customization File*. Lastly, navigate to the file folder you stored the OneNote customizations file in and click the *Open* button.

 Before you import a OneNote customizations file from another computer, it's a good idea to first export the existing menu settings as a backup.

56 Moving the cache file folder

In OneNote 2013/2016, the contents of all your currently open notebooks are stored on your local hard drive in the cache file folders. All changes you make to a notebook are done in those cached copies first. OneNote then automatically synchronizes everything to the actual notebook files. It doesn't matter if their storage location is on a local drive or in the cloud. If your computer is currently not connected to the internet the synchronization will be postponed until there is a connection again.

When you install OneNote, the location where OneNote stores the cache files is set to a place depending on the version of OneNote:

OneNote 2013:
C:\Users\<Username>\AppData\Local\Microsoft\One-Note\15.0\OneNoteOfflineCache_Files\ (subfolder)

C:\Users\<Username>\AppData\Local\Microsoft\One-Note\15.0\OneNoteOfflineCache.onecache (file)

OneNote 2016:
C:\Users\<Username>\AppData\Local\Microsoft\One-Note\16.0\cache\

Normally this location is perfectly fine. It should only be changed when some exceptional situation requires it, for example when the storage space on a SSD becomes too small. In that case you can move the cache to another location. This should be a fixed hard drive or another drive that is always available.
Moving the cache to another location goes like this:

1. Open *File – Options – Save & Backup*.

2. Locate the settings under *Cache file location*. Make sure you read the warning about selecting a drive that is always available, and then click the *Modify* button.

3. In the File Explorer dialog box, create or navigate to the desired folder location for the cache files. Click on the *Select* button.

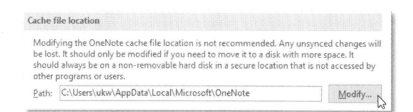

For the new cache folder location to become operational, you need to close OneNote and restart it.

This isn't exactly a move operation. OneNote actually rebuilds its cache in the new folder location from scratch by synchronizing data from all currently open notebooks. If you have very large notebooks, this may take quite a while. You'll also notice that the old cache folder isn't automatically deleted. Use File Explorer to delete the folder manually.

57 Multi-level undo

Made a mistake? No worries - just press **[Ctrl] + [Z]** or select **Undo** from the Quick Access Toolbar. How about seven mistakes? Select **Undo** seven times, or ... follow this tip.

Canceling the most recent action with the undo feature is quite common across Windows applications. It doesn't matter whether you deleted, added, moved or changed something – undo will repeatedly roll back to the previous state. The underlying mechanism for this is the undo buffer, a list of recent commands and edits. Every time an undo operation is requested, it jumps back one step through this list. In most programs, the undo buffer is invisible. This means there's no way to check up front exactly which action will be undone. There's also no way to execute multiple undo's in one go.

OneNote is an exception to this, thanks to the Office-wide implementation of the **Multi-level Undo** feature. The multi-level undo feature lets you cancel multiple actions in one swoop.

Although the feature is not included on any of the OneNote menus, you can quite easily add it to the Quick Start Menu or to the ribbon. While customizing either of these menus in the OneNote options, you will notice that there are two **Undo** commands listed under **Popular Commands**. The multi-level undo command is the one that has a tiny triangle icon. That triangle denotes the drop-down menu that will appear below or to the right of the command button on the menu.

The multi-level undo command actually consists of two buttons in one. The button with the arrow is the regular **Undo** command. The one with the triangle opens the undo history menu.

When you click on the drop-down triangle, a list of the most recent edit actions is displayed. Now, starting from the top of the list, point your mouse cursor at the actions that you want to undo. At the bottom of the list, the number of currently selected actions is displayed. Click your left mouse button to execute the multi-level undo.

 Note that it is not possible to select an individual action from the list, except for the top one.

58   Working offline

If you store your notebooks in the cloud and have an active internet connection, OneNote continually synchronizes changes that you make back to the notebook's online storage location. There may be quite a few reasons why you'd – temporarily – want to prevent changes from being synchronized: to save battery usage while working on a Windows tablet, for example. Another reason could be when you're working outside of your normal network and you'd like to reduce metered mobile data usage or to prevent your notes from being transmitted insecurely. OneNote's offline mode is also quite useful on board airplanes and at other places where internet access is prohibited.

 By "working offline" we don't mean that you store notebooks on your local hard drive, but that notes stored on OneDrive or SharePoint temporarily are not being synchronized.

The option to work offline is deeply hidden in the OneNote user interface: right-click on a notebook name, *select Notebook Sync Status* from the context menu and then turn *Sync manually* on or off. You can also add this command to the Quick Access Toolbar or to the ribbon. To find the command in the OneNote options for editing these menus, you need to set the command filter to *All Commands*. In the alphabetic command list, search for *Work Offline*, and add it to the menu.

If you select the Quick Access Toolbar to add this command, you'll notice that the command name *Work offline* will appear as text on the menu. To the left of the command name an active checkbox is displayed that allows you to enable and disable the feature.

If, on the other hand, you add **Work offline** to the ribbon, then this command behaves slightly differently: the background color of the command button is colorized (or grey) when the feature is enabled (= OneNote is offline).

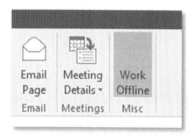

 OneNote offline mode is not the same as the One-Note cache, but offline mode does make use of the cache. On occasions when there's no internet connection, the OneNote cache stores changes to notes into files located on the local hard drive. This means that the OneNote cache is also active when **Work offline** is enabled.

59 Creating new pages without date/time stamp or title

Every note page in OneNote has a title, a horizontal line below it and a date and time stamp. Filling in a page title isn't mandatory. If you leave out a page title, OneNote will grab the first few words from the page and will use these as the page title for displaying it in the page list. By default, OneNote always adds the horizontal line and the date and time stamp. Of course you can delete these manually, but there's no built-in feature to create pages without a title.

Using the following tricks you can create new pages without a date and time stamp. If you like, you can even leave out the entire title field and the horizontal line. These tricks are based on OneNote page templates.

Pages with title, without date and time stamp:

- Create a new, empty page in the OneNote section where you want all of your pages to be without a date and time stamp.

- In the page header, select the date stamp and delete it.

- In the page header, select the time stamp and delete it.

- Your page is now ready to save as a future page template for this section. On the *Insert* menu in the *Pages* group, click on the blue *Page Templates* icon.

- On the right-hand side a task pane will open, titled *Page Templates*. At the very bottom of the task pane, click on the link *Save current page as a template*.

- The *Save As Template* dialog box will open. Give your new page template a name, for example "No date and time stamp".

- Put a checkmark in the box **Set as default template for new pages in the current section**.

- Click the **Save** button.

- Close the task pane by clicking on the X in the top-right corner.

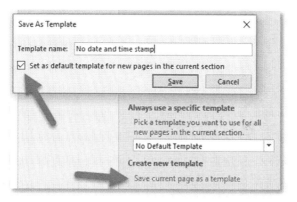

From now on, all pages in the current section will be created without a date and time stamp. This setting affects the current section only. To enable the same page template in another One-Note section, do the following:

1. Click on the tab for that section.

2. On the **Insert** menu in the **Pages** group, click the blue **Page Templates** button.

3. After the **Templates** task pane opens, look for the drop-down menu at the bottom of the task page, with the heading **Always use a specific template**. From this menu, select the page template you just created, for example "No date and time stamp".

4. Close the task pane by clicking on the **X** in the top-right corner.

Pages without title, horizontal line, date/time stamp

It's also possible to create pages without any page header at all: the page title, horizontal line and the date/time stamp are all suppressed. To create this page template, follow the same steps as for the page template "Pages with title, without date and time stamp", but instead of deleting the date and time stamp as indicated in steps 2 and 3, select *View – Hide Page Title*.

When saving your new page template, mark the option to apply it to the current section.

 This method has at least one drawback - it is now no longer possible to enter a page title. One approach could be to create a new note container at the top of the page and insert some text there. In the page tabs list, this text will then be used as a substitute for the page title. This is only a cosmetic solution though. When searching for the words in that 'title', OneNote will not rank the result under *In title*, but under *On page*, making the result less relevant.

60 Discovering the OneNote version number

When you're looking for a new feature, posting a question on the Microsoft Answers Forum or working on somebody else's computer, it can be really useful to know exactly which version of OneNote you're using. This has become even more relevant now that there are different desktop versions of OneNote for Windows. What's more, depending on your license, the OneNote you are working with may have a different build number and correspondingly may offer a different feature set.

To access information about your OneNote version, open *File – Account*. Focus on the section labeled *Product Information*, located on the right side of the account information panel. The exact version of Office is displayed right below the red Office logo. If you use the perpetual license of Office 2016, it may read "Microsoft Office Professional Plus 2016".

If you have an Office 365 license, this will be indicated, e.g. as "Subscription Product. Microsoft Office 365 ProPlus". Below the product name a list of your licensed Office component icons is displayed. Of course the OneNote icon is included. If you use the free version of OneNote 2016, the product name is

"Microsoft Office 2016 Home" with only the OneNote icon listed. The exact build number is displayed under **Office Updates**, right next to the **Update Options** button. In the text you can read more details about when and how updates will be installed. The exact version number is displayed here as well, for example, "16.0.6001.1038". For smaller updates, only the 4 digits to the right are likely to change.

The number "16" at the start refers to the 16th version of Microsoft Office – it does not refer to 2016. Office 2013 version numbers start with the number "15".

Information about whether you use the 32-bit or the 64-bit version of OneNote is displayed when you click on the **About OneNote** button, at the top of the information box. You may need that information for installing add-ins like Onetastic.

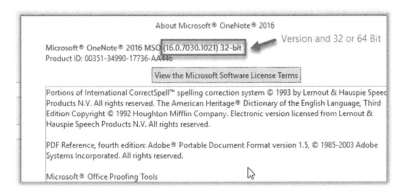

 OneNote for Windows 10 (the App Store or 'tile' version for Windows desktop, tablets and mobile phones) bears version numbers following a similar pattern, starting with "17". The version numbers for Apple devices is composed in a different manner, for example "15.24 [160702]". The part between square brackets indicates the release date.

61 Editing and sharing page templates

Editing and sharing OneNote page templates has always been a tedious job. Let's discuss these old methods first:

Editing page templates - the tedious way

1. Display the *Templates* task pane by selecting the blue *Page Templates* button from the the *Insert* menu tab.

2. Under *Add a page*, select any of the existing page templates from the list. This will create a new, empty page based on that page template.

3. Edit the page to reflect the desired changes.

4. Store your new page template under the old name using the task pane link *Save current page as a template*. Note that this creates a new page template that will be added to the bottom of your *My Templates* list. It does not overwrite the existing page template.

5. Delete your old page template by right-clicking the template name on the *Templates* task pane and selecting the *Delete* command from the context menu.

6. Close the task pane.

Sharing page templates - the tedious way

Up till now, this is how you'd share personal page templates:

1. Create a section in a shared notebook

2. Create a new page based on each individual OneNote page template that you'd like to share.

3. The recipients then open the notebook, and for each page in the section they save that page as a template.

My Templates.one - where OneNote stores page templates

Things get a lot simpler if you know that OneNote 2013/2016 stores all page templates in a separate OneNote notebook. The location of OneNote's templates notebook is not officially documented, but you can find it at:

C:\Users\<your username>\AppData\Roaming\ Microsoft\Templates\My Templates.one

You can open this notebook directly from OneNote through *File – Open – Computer – Browse*. This will open File Explorer. You can now paste the location of the My Templates.one notebook into the *File name* box.

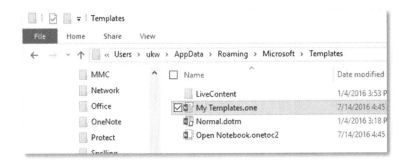

Of course you can also open File Explorer as a stand-alone application, navigate to the Templates folder and launch the My Templates.one notebook from there.

New-style template editing

Once the notebook has opened, it will appear as a regular OneNote notebook, named "Templates". This notebook contains a section named "My Templates". It is this section we are interested in. You can ignore the (mostly empty) section groups that appear. The section My Templates contains all the custom One-Note page templates you've defined before, appearing as page tabs in the page tabs list. You can now edit these pages. As with regular pages, any changes you make are immediately effective. There is no need to save the templates, because OneNote does this for you automatically.

New-style template sharing

Now, to share your page templates with others, you only need to copy the file **My Templates.one** and pass that on to them. On the recipient computer proceed as follows:

1. Open recipient's own **My Templates.one** file from their local hard drive.

2. Open the newly shared **My Templates.one** file they receive from you.

3. Now that both notebooks are open, copy the desired page templates from the shared notebook onto the recipient's own **My Templates.one** notebook.

 Of course the recipients can also replace the entire contents of their **My Templates.one** folder with the shared one.

 Note that these changes will affect newly created pages only. You cannot apply an updated page template onto an existing OneNote page. OneNote page templates should not be thought of as Word templates.

62 Setting rule lines as default page layout

The rule and grid lines available from *View – Rule Lines* instantly give your OneNote pages the look and feel of a real notebook. They are also most useful for drawing and digital inking, if you have a pen-enabled Windows PC. It makes sense to enable rule or grid lines on every page. There are two ways to do this - through a page template or using a OneNote option.

Enabling Rule lines through a page template

An obvious method to add rule or grid lines is to create a One-Note page template. To do so create an empty page and enable the desired style for rule or grid lines from the gallery at *View – Rule Lines*. Next, open the *Templates* task pane by clicking on the *Insert* menu tab and selecting the blue *Page Templates* command. Now click on the link *Save current page as a template* to give your template a name and *Set as default template for new pages in the current section*.

As you probably guessed, this method has advantages and disadvantages. The obvious advantage of a page template solution is that you can add other objects to it, such as images, tags and tables.

The disadvantage of a page template, firstly, is that it's rather tedious to make one. Another consideration is that a page template is active in only one section. If you want to use the same page template in another section, you'll have to manually activate it for that section.

There's another, much simpler method to create pages with rule or grid lines.

The 'always create pages with rule lines' option

On the *View* menu tab, under the same *Rule Lines* drop-down menu that holds the gallery of rule and grid lines, there is an option at the bottom called *Always Create Pages with Rule Lines*. If you select this option, a checkmark will appear to the left.

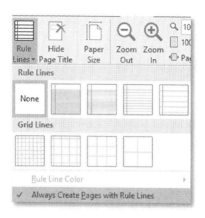

Another way to set the same option is by visiting *File – Options – Display*, checking the option *Create all new pages with rule lines* and clicking the *OK* button.

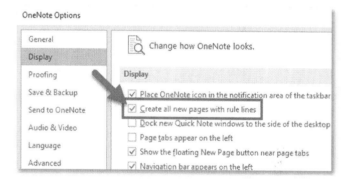

From now on, all pages that you create in any section in any notebook will have rule or grid lines as a page background. This behavior will continue until you remove the checkmark from the submenu or the OneNote options.

When you use this option, the next time you create a new page OneNote will use the rule or grid line variant that you selected last time. Note that only new pages are affected. The background layout of existing pages will not change. If you want to change the layout of existing pages, you can select a single page or select multiple pages at a time and change their rule or grid line in one go.

A disadvantage of this approach is that you cannot determine the rule line color in advance. OneNote will always use the blue color setting for pages it creates with this setting.

You can also add this command to your Quick Access Toolbar. Simply right-click *View – Rule Lines – Always Create Pages with Rule Lines* and select the option *Add to Quick Access Toolbar* from the context menu. This has the advantage that you can always see if this setting is enabled. In that case a check mark will appear on the Quick Access Toolbar to the left of the command name.

63 White grid on a colored background

Many OneNote users find pages with background colors and rule lines (or grids) easier to read and more appealing to the eye.

Adding a background color to a page is pretty straightforward - just open *View – Page Color*. A gallery of 16 background colors opens, along with an option to remove the page background color: *No Color*. These colors are consistent throughout OneNote. Because they match the colors for section tabs, you can have pages with a light-yellow page background under a yellow section tab.

On the same menu, the *Rule Lines* command contains the *Rule Line Color* feature. You can use this to add more spice to pages with colored backgrounds. Again, the familiar list with 16 color names appears, and also the option *<none>*. If you apply the *<none>* option on a page with a colored background, you'll get white lines on a colored background.

64 Applying the same background color to multiple pages

There is a way to apply page effects such as a specific background color or rule lines to multiple, or even to all, pages in a section at once. The secret is to select the pages in that section before applying the desired effect. If you only want to apply the effect to specific pages and not to all of them, then just select those individual pages in the page tabs list first.

To quickly select all pages in a section, click on the first page in the page tab list, then scroll down the page tabs list and Shift-click on the last page. If you prefer keyboard shortcuts, use **[Ctrl] + [Shift] + [A]**, **[Ctrl] + [A]**, **[Ctrl] + [A]**.

Now you can apply the desired effects, such as *Page Color*, *Rule Lines*, *Hide Page Title, etc.*

65 Modifying your author's initials

While you're editing a page, OneNote keeps track of which notes you edited at what time. When someone else views the same page, they will see your author's initials displayed in the margin to the right of your notes.

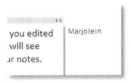

This way everyone with access rights to your notebook can keep track of who edited a page.

Instead of the usual initials **<FL>** for your first and last name, you can also use something else, such as your full first name, as an 'initial'. Here's how you set that up in OneNote 2013/2016:

1. Open *File – Options – General*.

2. Under *Personalize your copy of Microsoft Office*, put your first name (or something else) in the Initials field, to a maximum of 9 characters.

3. Save your settings with the *OK* button.

You need to restart OneNote for the new settings to take effect.

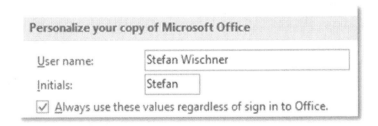

Any changes you make are applied to all Office programs on a single computer.

OneNote 2013/2016 is the only OneNote client that lets you change which initials it should use. Edits that you make from other OneNote clients will appear with your regular Windows initials .

If you use OneNote 2013/2016 on different Windows computers, you can decide to use the same initials on every computer, or make them distinct. If your initials are different, changes you make on another computer will appear as unread notes.

66 Relocating and resizing task panes

Task panes are dockable, multi-purpose dialog boxes implemented only in OneNote 2013/2016. By default, they appear to the right of the edit window after you click on a command. In OneNote, there are task panes for many purposes, such as

- Customize Numbering
- Find by Author
- Paper Size
- Password Protection
- Proofing Language
- Research
- Search Results
- Spelling
- Tag Summary
- Templates
- Thesaurus

There are several ways to customize task panes - you can resize them, undock them, reposition them and even dock a task pane to the left side of the screen. In Multiscreen-settings you may also put a task pane on another monitor. The custom position and size of a task pane are preserved between OneNote sessions.

As long as a task pane is docked to the OneNote window you can only change its width. Drag the left margin to do this.

Undocking and moving task panes

To undock a task pane so that you can reposition it, click on the task pane title and drag it away. It will become a floating window that you may position or resize at will. To dock it to its original position or to the left side, just move it to the right or left margin of the OneNote window. Alternatively double click on its title.

67 Adding a Speak feature to OneNote

As of Office 2010 Microsoft released a universal Text-to-Speech (TTS) feature across OneNote, Word, Outlook, Excel and Power-Point. Because the feature isn't available directly in the user interface, you'll need to add it yourself. There are three places where you can add the **Speak** command.

- To add Speak to the Ribbon, see our tip # 53 "Customizing the Ribbon". A good location for this command is a custom group on the Review menu tab.

- To add Speak to the Quick Access Toolbar, see our tip # 51 "The Quick Access Toolbar".

- To access Speak through the Mini Translator toolbar and have it read selected text in a foreign language, enable it from *Review – Translate – Mini Translator*. Once enabled, the Mini Translator pops up every time you select a piece of text with your mouse and release the mouse button. Hover your mouse cursor over the toolbar and click the *Play* (triangle) button to have OneNote pronounce the selected text.

68 Resetting the Tags list

If you accidentally modified the OneNote Tags list and need to restore the original one, you cannot do this from within OneNote itself. Tag customizations are stored in a file on your local hard drive, called **Preferences.dat**. That file preserves settings such as:

- recent search picks.
- recently used bullets and number formats.
- definitions for custom note tags.

You can restore the default OneNote tags list by following these steps:

1. Close OneNote.

2. In File Explorer open the correct folder for your version of OneNote:
   2013: c:\Users\<username>\AppData\Roaming\Microsoft\OneNote\15.0\
   2016: c:\Users\<username>\AppData\Roaming\Microsoft\OneNote\16.0\

3. Rename or delete the **Preferences.dat** file. We strongly suggest renaming it to something like **Preferences.bak**. This way you are able to copy / rename it back, in case some settings you did not think of are lost.

4. Restart OneNote.

Chapter 4 In and Out

Apart from writing or adding notes to a page directly, there are also some options to send content from other applications to OneNote. And sometimes content has to get out again – on paper or into a mail message.

69 Sending stuff to OneNote – the API confusion

A constantly increasing number of programs and services by Microsoft itself, as well as from 3rd party developers, are able to send content directly to your OneNote notebooks. But there are big differences.

Have you ever asked yourself why you can select a certain notebook as target for, let's say, an Outlook E-Mail but not for a web clipping?

The reason is that there are two different APIs. An API (Application Programming Interface) basically is a set of (more or less) publicly documented commands that programmers may use in their own applications to "talk" to OneNote. There may be commands to select a target notebook, to create a new section or page in it or to send data.

The older COM-API

Outlook, for example, is using the COM-API that was introduced with early OneNote versions and is still present in OneNote 2013/2016. Very simply put, if an application talks to that old COM-API, it communicates directly with OneNote 2013/2016 installed on your computer.

The main effect of this is that any currently open OneNote 2013/2016 notebook (or one left open when you last closed OneNote) can be selected as a target to send content to.

It doesn't matter where that notebook is stored, so notebooks on a LAN or your local hard drive are valid targets too.

You can tell that a program is using the COM-API by the dialog box which lets you choose the target location for any content. It looks like this:

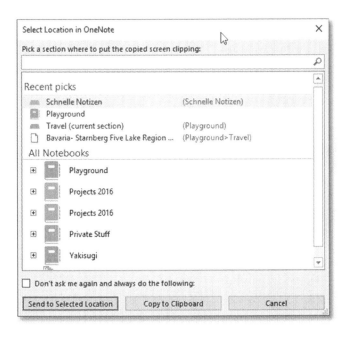

Programs / functions using the COM-API are:

- MS Outlook (for sending E-mail to OneNote).

- The OneNote virtual printer ("Print to OneNote").

- The Send to OneNote feature of Internet Explorer

- Screen clippings to OneNote using **[Win]** + **[Shift]** + **[S]**.

- Some 3rd party tools, like the screen capture application "SnagIt".

The modern Web-API

It's most likely that Microsoft won't develop the COM-API any further. Instead, they are using and advancing the modern alternative. Let's call it the Web-API (although this is technically not entirely correct). Programs and services using the Web-API don't talk to a locally installed OneNote application. In fact, OneNote doesn't need to be installed at all. Instead, the Web-API talks directly to the cloud server where notebooks are stored (OneDrive or OneDrive for Business). This means, of course, that notebooks stored locally, on a LAN share or SharePoint library, can't be used as a target for programs and services using the Web-API. Examples of those are:

- The Webclipper extensions for browsers (except the Send to OneNote feature of the Internet Explorer).

- The mail-to-OneNote-service (**me@onenote.com**).

- 3rd party programs and web services like IFTT (If This Then That).

- All existing or upcoming web and online services that are able to send content to (or fetch from) OneNote notebooks.

One advantage of using the Web-API is that any notebook on your account's cloud storage may be used as a target. It doesn't matter if it's been opened in a OneNote client before or not.

 Under *File – Options – Send to OneNote* you may define default locations for E-Mails, screen clippings or printouts. These options are valid for applications using the COM-API only, so you can't, for example, select the target location for websites saved by the web clipper extension. The *Web Content* setting is only used by the *Send to OneNote* feature of the Internet Explorer.

70   Scan to OneNote

OneNote 2013 has a feature that sadly has been removed from the 2016 version - to directly insert a scanned document into a OneNote page. If you use OneNote 2013, you can still find the scanner feature under *Insert – Scanned Image*.

Scanning as a fitness workout

Although useful, the OneNote 2013 scanning workflow is almost like a physical exercise program, at least with your scanner not being located within reach: selecting the right notebook and page, open OneNote Scan Image feature, set OneNote scan options, get up to walk to scanner, insert document into scanner, walk back to PC, click OneNote *Insert Scan* button, walk back to scanner once again, remove document, walk back to PC. If you have to do these steps multiple times in a row, it will quickly get on your nerves.

Scanners with OneNote support

Many manufacturers of modern scanners and so-called multi-function printers (MFP's) nowadays support scanning to Evernote directly from the scanner control panel, but unfortunately only a few vendors support sending scans directly to One-Note. Exceptions to this rule are Brother, Doxie, Epson and Fujitsu. However, there is another approach.

Email-To-OneNote as an alternative to scanning

Many scanners offer the capability to automatically output a scanned document to an email address. You can use this together with Microsoft's new Email-To-OneNote service. Anyone with a Microsoft ID or an Office 365 ID can forward documents to the email address **me@onenote.com**.

The advantage of the Email-To-OneNote approach is that you can quickly scan multiple documents in a row without needing to walk back and forth between your PC and your scanner. For quick access, your scanner may even allow saving the recipient address in its address book.

You may find that your scanner inserts the scanned document as a file attachment to the email and not as a printout image. That's easily fixed. In OneNote, right-click on the file icon and select *Insert as Printout* and you're done.

> The Email-To-OneNote service requires that the sender address correspond with a Microsoft ID or an Office 365 ID. On the Email-to-OneNote configuration page (**http://onenote.com/emailsettings**) you can define multiple email aliases from which the Email-To-OneNote service should accept messages. You can use these same email aliases in your scanner settings.

71 Printing multi-page (PDF) documents to OneNote

You can insert a document printout into OneNote in multiple ways, for example through *Insert – File Printout*, or by printing the file using the *Send to OneNote* virtual printer driver. By default, OneNote will combine all pages of a document printout into a single OneNote page.

OneNote offers a setting that affects how long documents get inserted as printout images into OneNote – combined into a single note page (the default) or as individual pages. You can find this setting in *File – Options – Advanced,* under the *Printouts* heading at the bottom of the Options panel. By default, this setting is off, which means that no matter how long the document is, its printout will always be inserted onto a single page.

That said, the setting description *Insert long printouts on multiple pages* is still a bit vague, as it immediately raises the question: *What is and what isn't a long printout?*

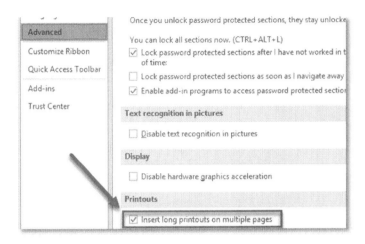

Some background explanation is clearly needed here. If you enable the setting, the cut-off point turns out to be at 10 pages. With the setting enabled, documents of 10 pages or more will be inserted as multiple pages.

No matter what the setting is, documents of 9 pages or less are always inserted as a single page. If you want to enforce that shorter documents are also split up into separate OneNote pages, there are two rather cumbersome work-arounds:

- Manually create new pages for every image in the printout, then drag&drop every image onto its own page.

- Edit the original document or use an external utility such as PDF Split & Merge to artificially bring the total number of pages in the document to 10. After printing to OneNote, you'll have to remove the superfluously inserted pages.

72 Alternative ways to share notes

Sometimes the standard method of sharing a OneNote notebook in its entirety is too much of a good thing: it could be you just want to share specific pages, a specific section, or only the notebook as it exists today and not in its future state.

Another reason to consider alternative sharing methods may be that the notebook is simply not located on a shared OneDrive, SharePoint or LAN resource location.

Of course you can send OneNote pages by email (possible only if the sender has got Outlook installed). It's just that in this case he would get the note content inside the message body.

Other methods you may want to consider are the export formats MHTML, PDF / DOC(X) and ONE / ONEPKG. Let's take a closer look at each of these methods.

MHTML export format (.MHT)

The export format MHTML, with file extension MHT, is a format used to archive complete web pages. In addition to the HTML code, an MHTML archive also contains external objects referred to from the HTML code, such as images.

A clear advantage of using the MHTML export format is that the original page layout remains intact and that the recipient doesn't need to use OneNote to view the pages. But currently only Internet Explorer is able to open MHT-files without problems. In Google Chrome images are often missing and Firefox needs an add-on to open MHT. Microsoft Edge does not support MHT-files yet.

To create an MHTML archive in OneNote, first select one or more pages that you want to export in the page tabs list or open *File – Export* directly. Select *Single File Web Page (*.mht)* as the output format and click on the *Export* button. Provide the name of the .mht file and click on the *Save* button.

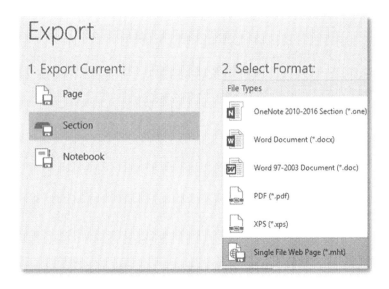

If you want to export an entire section, you can also right-click on the section tab and select the **Export** command from the context menu. Provide the name of the .mht file and click on the **Save** button.

PDF / DOC(X) document export formats

The obvious advantage of using PDF is that this is a very common output format for which the recipient only requires a free PDF reader. It's also important to know that you can export an entire notebook to PDF. This is not possible with MHTML archives and also not possible with export as Word documents.

In both cases, PDF and Word DOC, the orignal layout of the note page may not be preserved. All printable content will be there but possibly not in the same arrangement as in OneNote.

To export OneNote pages as Word documents, the Word application needs to be installed. Users of the free version of OneNote 2016 will notice that that option is missing from their Export menu. According to Microsoft, this is because the export feature requires specific components that are only available with MS Office installed .

ONE / ONEPKG export formats

The ONE and ONEPKG export formats are OneNote-proprietary formats. These are the most suitable formats to export one or multiple pages (ONE), a section (ONE), and even an entire notebook (ONEPKG).

A ONEPKG file is, in fact, a complete, zipped clone of an existing notebook. Each time a recipient opens the ONEPKG file, a new notebook is generated based on the originally exported one. In that sense, a ONEPKG is considered a notebook template file.

To export in ONE / ONEPKG format, first select one or more pages in the page tabs list. You can also open *File – Export* directly. From the *1. Export Current* column select the scope of your export (page, section or notebook) and from the *2. Select Format* column select the ONE or ONEPKG output format.

The obvious disadvantage of the ONE and ONEPKG output formats is that the recipient needs to have the Office-Version of OneNote 2013/2016 for a convenient way to open those files.

73 Hosting a notebook on Docs.com

Docs.com is a fairly recently launched document hosting service offered by Microsoft. You can also use it to host OneNote notebooks so that others can create a copy of them. You can read more about it in our next tip.

Apart from the traditional ways of sharing a OneNote notebook, Microsoft now provides a new, web-based method specifically tailored to distributing notebooks to larger audiences, called Docs.com. This is a document hosting platform that you can use to upload and host any of your OneNote notebooks so that other people can clone them for their own use. There are two procedures you should know about - how to host a notebook, and how others can get a copy of that notebook.

Hosting a OneNote notebook on Docs.com

1. Prepare your notebook for publication, using the tip #40 about cleaning up a notebook before sharing it.

2. On Docs.com sign in with your Microsoft or O365 ID.

3. Click on the *Publish* button.

4. From the dialog box *Share what you love*, select *One-Note*.

5. Docs.com will now create an alphabetic list of all notebooks that it can find across all of your document folders on OneDrive (Microsoft ID) or OneDrive for Business (Office 365 ID).

6. Select the notebook you want to host and click on the *Open* button. You can only select one notebook at a time.

7. Docs.com will now take a few seconds to fetch the notebook from your file storage account and upload it. In the meantime, you can edit the notebook details: title, author name, description, a background image,

visibility (public or limited), a usage license (e.g. Creative Commons Attribution), comments allowed, tags and language.

8. Use the **Share** button to create a shortened link for your notebook. You can forward this link to specific people. You can also post the link on social media so that anonymous recipients can copy your notebook.

Copying a OneNote notebook hosted on Docs.com

After you share the shortened link to a notebook hosted on Docs.com, any recipient can open the link. He will see a button labeled **Get Notebook**. After clicking on it, a copy of the notebook will be created in the recipient's own OneDrive or OneDrive for Business account. This may take a few minutes. After that, the recipient can click the red **View in Browser** button to open the new notebook in OneNote Online or click on the **Open it in the OneNote app** to open it in OneNote on the desktop. Note that this is a copy of the original notebook. Any changes that you make to the original notebook are not propagated onto the copies that other people make of that notebook and vice versa.

Updating a OneNote notebook hosted on Docs.com

If for some reason you need to change the details or even refresh a hosted OneNote notebook, you can do so as follows:

1. Locate the notebook document thumbnail in your Docs.com account.

2. Point your mouse cursor onto the document thumbnail. A menu will slide open with an **Edit** button. This will open a dialog box that allows you to edit the details of the OneNote notebook.

3. Adjust any of the details.

4. You can now **Save** the settings, or select **Re-upload**.

74 Convert all handwriting on a page

Handwritten notes may be easily converted into printed text. Just select the ink object you want to convert. You may use the selection rectangle or the *Lasso Select* tool from the *Draw* Menu. Right click on the object and chose *Ink to text*. The handwritten text will be replaced by computer text.

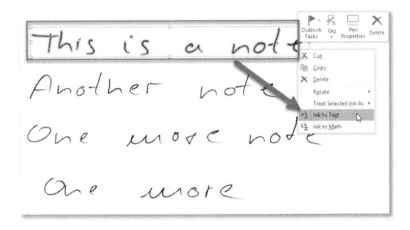

Did you know that there is an easier way to convert all handwritten notes on a page at once? Just don't select anything and right click somewhere on the page. There is no *Ink to text* command in the menu now. *Click on Convert Ink* instead. This pops up a new menu where you select *Ink to text*. This exchanges all recognized handwritten notes on the page into computer text.

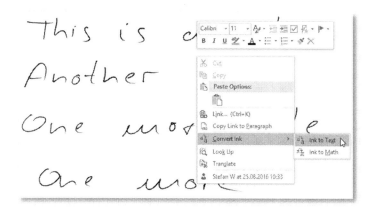

The converted text:

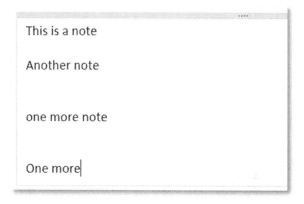

75 Sending handwritten notes to MS Word

If you want to copy a handwritten note to Word you could of course use the clipboard. That method would preserve the note as an ink object. However, if you use OneNotes Export to Word option instead, all handwritten notes will immediately be transferred to "normal" text.

1. In OneNote, select one or more pages in the page tabs list. You can also skip this part and select an entire section in step 2.

2. Open *File – Export*. Under the heading *1. Export Current*, select either *Page* or *Section*. If you have selected multiple pages, all of them will be exported into one Word document.

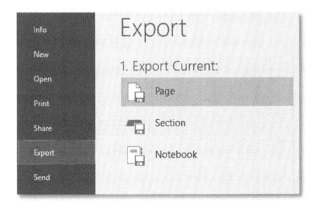

3. Under the heading *2. Select Format*, select a Word-Format, e.g. *Word Document (*.docx)*.

2. Select Format:

File Types

- OneNote 2010-2016 Section (*.one)
- Word Document (*.docx)
- Word 97-2003 Document (*.doc)
- PDF (*.pdf)

4. Click on the ***Export*** button.

5. If you now open the Word document you just created, you'll notice that the digital ink has automatically converted to machine-readable text.

Export in Word format is possible only with the "paid" (Office) version of OneNote. It requires specific components that only get installed if the entire Office suite is available. This means that Export to Word will not work with the free version of OneNote 2016 that you can download from onenote.com.

76 Inserting files in OneNote pages

OneNote can be used to insert and attach files of any type. This makes it very tempting to use OneNote as a document and file management application. Before you try to do that, there are a few things you should know.

As Attachement

A file attachment in OneNote is comparable to an email attachment. An integral copy of the original document is inserted into the note page, and from there into the notebook storage location, for example OneDrive. The connection with the original file is lost – if you change the embedded version, the original file remains intact and vice versa.

This behavior seems illogical if you want to use OneNote as a document management system. If you are looking for a way to archive documents, then it does make sense.

There are two ways to add a file attachment to a note page:

- using Drag & Drop from File Explorer straight onto the note page. Before the file is inserted, a prompt appears to let you choose between *Attach File* and *Insert Printout*.

- from OneNote, using *Insert – File Attachment*.

Attached files can be opened using the associated Windows application by double-clicking on the file icon.

Inserting file printouts

The virtual printer driver **Send To OneNote**, available for OneNote 2013 and 2016, allows you to insert a printout from any type of file that can be printed. That includes printing text documents, PDFs, presentations, diagrams and many other file types – straight into OneNote. The printout is inserted as a pure bitmap graphic that can be instantly searched thanks to OneNote's OCR technology. The accuracy of the text recognition may be lower if you use complex layouts, insufficient contrast or fancy type-faces. Naturally, the file printout feature is useful only for archiving purposes. Here are three ways to insert a file printout:

1. From any Windows program, use that program's print feature and select **Send to OneNote 2013/2016** as the destination. The print dialog box may offer various print options, such as orientation, paper size and print qual-ity. After clicking on the **Print** button, a dialog box **Select Location in OneNote** will appear to specify the destina-tion page or section.

2. From OneNote itself, select **Insert – File Printout**. A File Explorer dialog box will let you select one or more files that you'd like to insert. Your computer needs to have a program installed with a printing feature for that spe-cific file type e.g. to insert a PDF file, you need to have a PDF viewer installed. The printout will be inserted into the current page. There is a difference compared to the previous method - above the inserted printout a special file object is inserted with a file icon corresponding to the inserted file type. This file icon links to a *copy* of the original file. If you right-click on this file icon, a context menu appears that provides access to some file related features like **Open**, **Save As...**, **Refresh** or **Copy a link** to the original file.

3. The third way to insert a file printout is by dragging & dropping one or more files from File Explorer onto a OneNote page. Select *Insert Printout* from the dialog box. This will result in the same type of inserted file as the previous method, including the file object and context menu. Make sure you have a file viewer installed for the inserted file type. If you select multiple files before you drag & drop, the files will be inserted as attachments, not as printouts.

Inserting a hyperlink to a file

From a document management perspective, inserting a hyperlink to a file is the best method, You are not creating a copy of an original file, but only inserting a named link to it. Links take much less space than file attachments and file printouts, making synchronization with OneDrive and other file storage locations much quicker.

Past versions of OneNote offered a third option when dragging and dropping files from the Explorer, called *As Link.* As of OneNote 2013, Microsoft has dropped this option. There is a work-around that still allows you to insert a hyperlink to a file:

1. Select *Insert – Link* or press [Ctrl] + [K].

2. In the *Link* dialog box, right next to the empty address field, look for the yellow folder icon. Click this button.

3. The next dialog box, called *Link to File*, lets you select a file using File Explorer. Confirm your selection by clicking on the *Open* button.

4. You're now back at the *Link* dialog box. Note that the *Text to display* field has been populated with the file name. You can adjust this as you see fit. Confirm once again with a click on the *OK* button. A hyperlink is now inserted at the cursor location.

In OneNote 2013 and 2016 you can embed Excel and Visio files. This feature – only available for users who have a license to use these programs – is something of a hybrid of the three methods described above: it inserts a copy of the original file and shows a preview of the file content. When you click on the **Edit** button, a copy of the original file is being edited – not the original. As soon as you **Save** the file, the preview in OneNote gets refreshed. If you want these changes to be applied to the original file, you'll have to deliberately use the **Save As** feature in Excel or Visio for that. If you want to edit the original file directly, right-click on the file icon and select **Open Original** from the context menu.

77 Printing an entire notebook

In OneNote 2013/2016, printing a couple of pages or a whole section is no problem. Printing an entire notebook, however, is not possible – unless you apply the following trick. First export your notebook to a PDF file, using **File – Export**. Under **1. Export Current**, select **Notebook**. Under **2. Select Format**, choose **PDF**. Then click on the **Export** button.

You can now open your preferred PDF viewer and use its built-in printing feature to get the paper version of your OneNote notebook. Note that for technical reasons the formatting of the PDF / printed pages may not always look as expected.

78 OneNote's sticky notes - Quick Notes

When working with OneNote, you normally open the notebook, section and page where you want to write your notes. But what if you have no time to think about this hierarchy and just want to quickly jot something down? That's when the fairly unknown Quick Notes feature comes in.

Quick Notes are a fast way to create an empty, unfiled note that's available even when OneNote itself isn't running. For Quick Notes to work, a small memory-resident program called **Send To Onenote** needs to be running. By default, it auto-starts with Windows. How **Send To OneNote** behaves depends on your version of OneNote.

Quick Notes in OneNote 2013

If you have OneNote 2013 installed, **Send To OneNote** appears as a shortcut on the Windows Taskbar. It looks like a OneNote program icon with a tiny pair of scissors. If you click on that icon or press **[Win] + [N]**, a small pane with three purple tiles will pop up from the taskbar. You can then simply press **[N]** to open a quick note. An alternative keyboard shortcut is **[Win] + [Alt] + [N]**.

Quick Notes in OneNote 2016

For OneNote 2016 Microsoft removed that extra window from the taskbar. **Send To OneNote** appears as an icon in the Notification area (System Tray) instead. One function (Send to OneNote) has been removed, but creating a Quick Note by pressing **[Win] + [N]** (without an additional **[N]**) is still there.

Look and feel of Quick Notes

No matter which version of OneNote you use, Quick Notes behave in the same, distraction-free way. A Quick Note in OneNote is basically just a OneNote page with some special properties. It has a pink background, most UI-elements (page header, ribbon, QAT...) are hidden and it stays on top of other windows.

If you want to move your note out of the way, click on the x in the top-right corner. OneNote will automatically save your note.

Even though most of the menu controls are hidden from a Quick Note, in fact, they are still accessible with a single click. To quickly access all the features on the ribbon and Quick Access Toolbar, click on the triple-dot title bar at the top. The double-sided, diagonal arrow in the top-right corner of a Quick Note lets you switch to **Normal View**. Once you click on that arrow, all elements of the OneNote user interface are restored.

Quick Notes storage location

Quick Notes are always stored in the same location. You can access this aptly named **Quick Notes** section through a link listed at the very bottom of the notebook navigation list. Check and change where this Quick Notes section is stored by opening **File – Options – Save & Backup**. The current Quick Notes location is listed under the **Save** options group. By clicking on the **Modify** button, you can designate any section of any OneNote notebook as your preferred Quick Notes section. Note that you can name the section any way you like – the name 'Quick Notes' isn't mandatory. Press the **Select** button to confirm the new location, and press **OK** to save your settings.

79 Email To OneNote from any address

Apart from entering notes in a OneNote page directly, you can also send your notes to OneNote by using the **Email To OneNote** service. This service consists of an email address to which you forward existing email messages or send newly created ones. The subject field of the email message becomes the title of your OneNote page. It's important to know that – very unlike other services that support custom email addresses – the email address implemented by Email To OneNote is one and the same for all OneNote users: **me@onenote.com**.

Email To OneNote works out of the box with Microsoft IDs and Office 365 IDs. You can refine your Email To OneNote configuration by visiting **https://www.onenote.com/EmailToOneNote**.

Here's a nice benefit of the Email To OneNote service that many people are not aware of - any URL that you include in the body of an email message automatically gets expanded into a full-blown article in OneNote. What's inserted is both the article as text and a full-page screenshot as image. Another benefit is that you can use Email To OneNote from any sender address. That said, there are a number of limitations to this service. Here's what you need to know:

- The notebook to which you send your messages needs to be stored on either OneDrive or OneDrive for Business. This means you cannot use a locally stored notebook as you can when forwarding email messages with the OneNote add-in for Microsoft Outlook.

- With every message you send, you can specify a different destination notebook *section name* at the end of the message subject field. More about this in the next tip ("Using Outlook rules...").
The destination *notebook name*, however, needs to be specified up front at **www.onenote.com/EmailSettings** and you can only choose a single notebook for all messages that you forward. You cannot vary the destination notebook for individual messages (yet?).

- All messages sent to **me@onenote.com** need to originate from the email address connected to the Microsoft ID or Office 365 ID that you used to sign up for the service. In other words, it is the *email sender address* that determines to whose notebook a message will be sent.

Now, Microsoft does allow you to specify alias email addresses that are also accepted as the message sender by using Outlook.com - Microsoft's web-based email service that you can use with a Microsoft ID. Alias email addresses are a key component in a trick that allows you to use any email address to send notes to a OneNote notebook.

How to use Email To OneNote from any address

1. Create an Outlook.com alias email address, as follows: Sign in to **outlook.com** with your Microsoft ID and open the *Options* panel from the cog wheel drop-down menu in the top-right corner. Now, select the *Create an Outlook.com* alias option and enter the desired alias. If your Microsoft ID is **cathysmith@outlook.com**, an alias could

be **onenote-cathysmith@outlook.com**. Note that this alias does not have an inbox of its own. Instead, all messages sent to the alias address are automatically sent to the email address associated with your Microsoft ID.

2. From the Outlook.com cog wheel menu, open Manage Rules. Click on the New button. You will see four boxes. From the condition drop-down menu (box 1), select Recipient contains. In the next box (2), specify your alias email address. From the action drop-down menu (3), select Forward to. In the last box (4) type me@onenote.com.

From now on, any email message that you send to the alias email address will be automatically forwarded to the Email To OneNote service, independent of which email address you (or someone else) use to send the message.

A possible disadvantage of creating OneNote pages in this manner is that the originating sender's email address is no longer visible.

Any alias email address you create should be kept private, otherwise anyone knowing it could control what content appears in your OneNote notebook. Should it inadvertently happen that your alias email address becomes known, then you can easily delete it and create a new alias.

80 Using Outlook Rules with OneNote

A nice way to archive specific email messages is provided by the OneNote add-in for Outlook. This add-in automatically gets installed with the full versions of Office and Office 365 and adds a **OneNote** button to the **Move** command group on the **Home** menu tab in Outlook. The same command is also available from the context menu that appears if you right-click on a message in a folder list like **Inbox**.

Unfortunately Outlooks rule assistant does not offer a "Send to OneNote" action in the Outlook Rules Wizard – it simply does not "talk" to the add-in. That's really a pity because it would have been very nice to automatically forward messages to specific OneNote sections depending on the originating sender or depending on words in the subject.

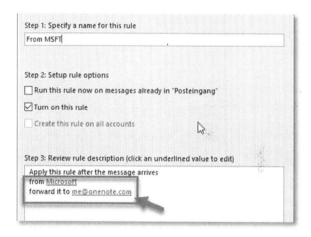

Nonetheless, you can use the Email To OneNote service (see previous tip) to accomplish the same result. Simply forward your messages from the email address associated with your Microsoft ID or with your Office 365 to **me@onenote.com**. You can also use an alias email address. Of course, all features of Outlook Rules are available to you while defining a new rule. Note that the target notebook has to be stored in the cloud for this.

81 Using Outlook Quick Steps

A relatively new feature in the Email To OneNote service is that with each email message you forward to it, you can specify the OneNote destination section. To do so, simply append an "@" character to the message subject, followed by the desired One-Note section name.

Unfortunately, the previously explained Outlook Rules Wizard doesn't allow you to programmatically alter the message subject field so that a message could be forwarded to specific notebook sections depending on its content. There are two work-arounds here: you can rather laboriously create a Visual Basic macro for Outlook and have the Rules Wizard execute that script or you can use Quick Steps.

With an Outlook Quick Step, you can semi-automatically process email messages. Other than through Outlook Rules, Quick Steps can't be triggered automatically by an event or condition. You must start them manually with a simple mouse click or keyboard shortcut. What makes Quick Steps special is that it can alter the message subject field, thus allowing you to send a message to a specific section. Here's how you need to go about it:

1. From the *Home* menu tab, select *Create New* from the *Quick Steps Gallery*.

2. In the **Edit Quick Step** dialog box, select *Action – Forward* (under the *Respond* action group).

3. In the *To* field, type **me@onenote.com**.

4. Click on the *Show Options* link.

5. Edit the *Subject* field so that it reads *<Subject> @<section name>* (the < and > characters are not needed).

6. If desired, select one of the available keyboard shortcuts (**[Ctrl]** + **[Shift]** + **[1]** - **[9]**).

7. Click on the *Finish* button.

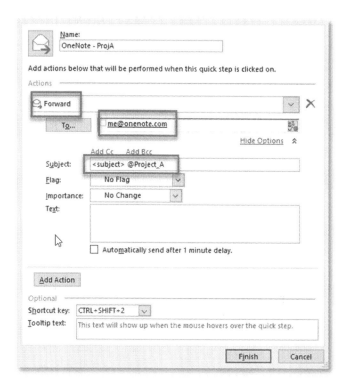

 The section name that you specify in the message subject field needs to exist in the default notebook specified in the settings of the Email To OneNote service. If the section name doesn't exist yet, the service will automatically create a new section with the indicated name.

 Like any action involving the send to **me@onenote.com** mechanism, the target notebook has to be stored in the cloud. Notebooks located on your PC or a network share won't be recognized.

82 Sending multiple e-mails to OneNote

We already discussed the Outlook add-in that lets you send a selected e-mail message to OneNote from the context menu or a ribbon command. This used to work for multiple messages as well, until Microsoft changed the behavior of the add-in with a patch on Outlook 2013.

Now when you select more than one message and right-click to open the context menu, the **OneNote** command is missing.

Here comes the good news: It is still possible to send multiple e-mail messages to a OneNote page in one go. Although the context menu entry is gone, you can still find a **OneNote** command in the **Move** section of the **Home** menu. Clicking on that will send all selected messages to a notebook/section that you can select in the upcoming dialog box.

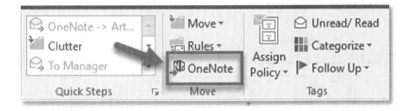

 The target notebook has to have been open when you last used OneNote. OneNote itself doesn't have to be running when you send the message.

 If you use this command alot, you may add the One-Note command to the Quick Access toolbar. Just right-click on the OneNote icon and select **Add to Quick Access Toolbar**.

83   Pasting slides from PowerPoint

The **Send to OneNote** and **Insert File Printout** features were invented to quickly send content from other programs to a One-Note page. These image printout methods also work with Microsoft PowerPoint. Still, they have several disadvantages: the printout images generated in OneNote have alot of superfluous white space at the margins. Because they are sent straight to the page canvas, the images are also hard to select and manipulate.

The secret here is to copy the slide thumbnails from the PowerPoint presentation and paste these into OneNote. This method has several advantages:

- No superfluous white space around the actual images.

- All images are combined into a single container.

- All images are in a smaller, more attractive size.

- All images are nicely aligned.

- The images can be easily manipulated and moved.

Here are the steps:

1. Open the PowerPoint presentation and select **View – Normal**. Thumbnails of each of the slides should now appear on the left.

2. Click on one of the slide thumbnails.

3. Press **[Ctrl] + [A]** to extend the selection to all slides, or select multiple individual slides using **[Ctrl]**-click.

4. Copy the thumbnails to the Windows clipboard with **[Ctrl] + [C]**.

5. Switch to your OneNote window and paste the selection into a page with **[Ctrl] + [V]**.

84 Suppress URLs from pasted content

Whenever you copy and paste some content from a program like Word, and the source file (the document in this case) is stored on OneDrive or OneDrive for business, a lengthy web URL is also pasted onto the OneNote page. This is pointing to the origin of the source file.

It's very likely that this behavior was never intended by Microsoft (or was it? You never know). It seems that OneNote is interpreting the source of the clipboard content as a web page. The good news is you can easily switch this behavior off.

1. Open *File – Options*.

2. From the left menu select *Advanced*.

3. In the *Edit* section uncheck the option *Include link to source when pasting from the web*.

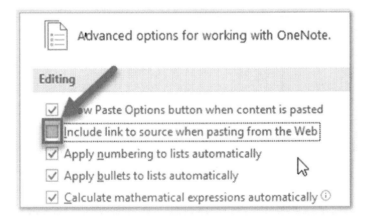

Chapter 5   Security and Privacy

If you store more crucial information in OneNote than shopping lists or web articles to read later, security and privacy should be a concern for you. This chapter is about backing up and restoring notes, as well as keeping them for your eyes only.

85   Configuring automatic backups

OneNote has a built-in backup mechanism that not only covers local notebooks, but also the ones stored on SharePoint, on OneDrive and on OneDrive for Business. All versions of OneNote 2013/2016 for Windows offer this backup feature, including the free version. However, the default backup settings require a few tweaks as the default settings don't make much sense.

1. Open *File – Options – Save & Backup*.

2. Under the *Save* heading, select the row *Backup Folder* and modify it to choose a different location, preferably on an external drive. Note that your existing backups are not automatically moved to the new location.

3. By default OneNote creates backups only every 2 weeks. Depending on your use of OneNote, this interval may be much too long. Adjust it according to your needs under *Backup* with the setting *Automatically back up my notebook at the following time interval*.

4. If you want, you can adjust how many versions to keep by changing the number next to *Number of backup copies to keep*. After that number is reached, the oldest backup will be overwritten.

5. You may at any time force a manual backup:
   Click on the button *Back Up All Notebooks Now*.

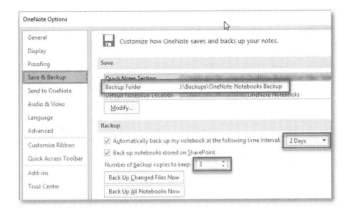

 OneNote only backs up notebooks that are currently open and synchronized to your local PC.

 Be careful of having multiple notebooks with identical names (which is possible when stored in different locations). OneNote stores all backups by name in a single, non-hierarchical backup folder. This means that the backup for one notebook will inevitably overwrite another identically-named backup without warning.

86 Restoring a backup

It happened: You accidentally deleted or overwrote important information and you need to turn back time. Don't panic – if you made sure to heed our previous tip to tweak the settings for automatic backups, chances are that you'll be up and running again in no time. Here are the steps to restore a notebook backup in OneNote 2013/2016 (Office and free versions).

1. Open the *File* menu tab to reach the backstage view, called *Notebook Information*. In the top-right corner, click on the button *Open Backups*.

2. In File Explorer open the folder with the notebook name you'd like to restore. OneNote will now display the individual sections for that notebook. Use **[Ctrl]**-click to mark individual sections for restoring. To mark a whole range of sections, use **[Shift]**-click. Confirm your selection by clicking on the *Open* button.

3. The sections that you selected are immediately opened and available through a special area newly added to the bottom of the notebook navigation list, called *Open Sections*. This compartment behaves just like a regular OneNote notebook, except that the restored sections are *read-only*.

4. To work with the restored sections, they need to be copied to a notebook to which you have both read and write access. If the destination notebook doesn't exist yet, you'll need to create it before copying sections to it. You can only *copy* restored sections, not *move* them. This is because during the backup process the sections are marked as read-only.

5. One by one, right-click on a section tab and select the ***Move or Copy*** command from the context menu. Select the desired destination notebook and click on the ***Copy*** button.

6. You'll want to rename each restored section as they carry the date they were last backed up in the section name.

To restore an entire notebook, you'll need to build it back up by restoring individual sections one by one. Unfortunately it isn't possible to restore an entire notebook in one go.

87 Backup using ONEPKG files

Besides the OneNote built-in method to create scheduled back-ups, there is another way to manually create an integral copy of a OneNote notebook in the so-called ONEPKG format, also known as OneNote Package. A notebook exported as an ONEPKG file contains all section groups, sections, pages and attached files archived into a single file. Originally invented to allow the transfer of a OneNote notebook from one computer to another, ONEPKG files are also perfectly suitable as a backup solution.

It makes no difference if your notebooks are stored locally or on a LAN, on SharePoint, on OneDrive or on OneDrive for Business. Here's how to create a OneNote packaged file:

- Open *File – Export.*

- Under the heading *Export Current,* select *Notebook*.

- Under *Select Format,* select *OneNote Package (*.onepkg).*

- Click on the *Export* button. Navigate to the desired storage location and confirm by clicking on the *Save* button.

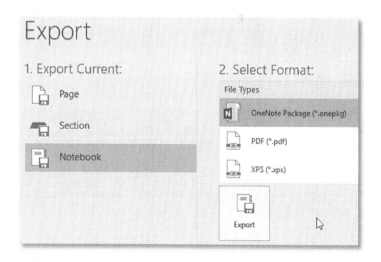

At any point the packaged file can be opened just like any locally stored notebook: just open *File – Open – Computer*, select the ONEPKG file and click on the *Open* button. This will create a copy of the original notebook in the exact state it was in when the packaged file was created. You can also open File Explorer from the Windows start menu and launch the ONEPKG file from there by double clicking on it. In both cases you will be asked for the name of a new notebook to import the content of the ONEPKG file into.

 Creating a OneNote package in this way also works from the free OneNote 2016 version. However, opening a ONEPKG from the free version results in an error message, prompting you to install a paid version to proceed. No worries - you can still get it to work with the next tip.

88 Opening ONE and ONEPKG with the free OneNote 2016

If you have the (paid) Office version of OneNote 2013/2016, you can simply open exported **ONE** and **ONEPKG** files by double clicking on them in File Explorer. If there are several **ONE** files (these are actually OneNote sections) in a folder AND in addition, there is a file with the extension **.ONETOC2** present, clicking on any **ONE** file will open all of them, forming a complete notebook again. But if you try either of these with the free version of OneNote 2016, you will just get error messages.

 "Free version of OneNote" means the desktop app called "OneNote 2016" that you can download for free from onenote.com. With the also free Universal App "OneNote" that is installed with Windows 10, these tips won't work.

These tricks will let you open **ONE** and **ONEPKG** files in the free OneNote 2016 as well:

• To open **ONE** files, simply rename or remove the .ONETOC2 file. That way you can open section files one by one. Importing a complete notebook in one go is not possible.

• To open a **ONEPKG,** you need to understand that this is nothing other than a ZIP file with a different extension. You can open it with a good packaging program like **7-Zip** or **WinZip** (the Windows Explorer won't do). After unpacking you get the common OneNote file structure, including **ONE** files that can be opened as described above.

These methods are not as convenient as if you were using the full version of OneNote 2016, but at least it works to import local OneNote files at all.

89   Retrieving deleted notes

If you accidentally deleted only a section, or just a couple of notes, restoring a backup may not be necessary. For every individual notebook, OneNote maintains a separate Recycle Bin. The bin temporarily holds on to deleted pages and sections for 60 days – after that they are erased for good. Here's how to find and restore your deleted notes:

1. In the notebook navigation list, find the desired notebook. Then right-click on the notebook name and select **Notebook Recycle Bin** from the context menu. If you are looking for the recycle bin of the currently open notebook, then open the **History** menu tab and click on the **Recycle Bin** command icon. Inside the notebook a view is opened of the hidden section group **One-Note_RecycleBin**. It's structured just like a regular section group with section tabs and a page tabs list.

2. Locate the section or page you'd like to undelete and right-click it. Next, select **Move or Copy** from the context menu and pick the desired destination notebook. Confirm your action by clicking on the **Move** or **Copy** button.

3. Just like exiting a regular section group, you can exit the Recycle Bin by clicking on the curved green arrow right next to the notebook name.

If for any reason you'd like to permanently erase all deleted sections and pages, then you can do so via the **History** menu tab. Click on the command button with the label **Notebook Recycle Bin** and select **Empty Recycle Bin** from the drop-down menu.

90 Auto-lock password-protected sections

In all OneNote clients password protection is done at the level of individual sections only. You cannot lock an entire notebook, a section group, or selected individual pages. To activate password protection, right-click on the section tab, select **Password Protect This Section** and enter a password. Next time anyone wants to open that section, they will be required to enter that same password.

So far so good, but what if a password-protected page is open on your computer and you need to quickly move away from your desk? No problem: you can instantly lock your password-protected sections with the keyboard shortcut **[Ctrl] + [Alt] + [L]**. This command affects not just the currently open section, but *all* password-protected sections in the notebooks you have open.

It's easy to forget locking your sections. That's why OneNote does this automatically for you if you haven't edited a section for a number of minutes. You can set this time in the program settings, under *File – Options – Advanced*. Under the *Password* heading you'll see a drop-down box to set the number of minutes.

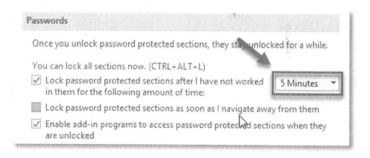

If you want, you can disable the auto-locking feature completely. Simply remove the checkmark for the option. You can also enable the option to lock the current section as soon as you switch to another section.

91 Password protection is partially ineffective!

This tip is primarily a warning. It's true you can password-protect sensitive data in OneNote 2013/2016, but any files that you attach (including PDFs and images) are being saved without any encryption. This applies not just to the original copy of your notebook stored locally, on a LAN drive, on OneDrive, OneDrive for Business or SharePoint, but also to the cached copy of that notebook stored in the OneNote cache folder on your hard drive.

This means that anyone who has access to your PC and knows their way around a computer could access all embedded files and images in your OneNote notebooks, whether you've encrypted the notebook sections or not.

There is no workaround for this issue, except to block access to your PC in another way.

It may seem appealing to programmatically erase the cache folder on OneNote exit, but this has the major drawback that your notebooks will take much longer to load when you re-open the program.

92 Last Resort: Backup as PDF

In this chapter we showed you several methods to back up your notebooks and keep your valuable data safe from technical harms and human errors.

But all these methods have one thing in common: They all create backups in a format that only OneNote can understand. So what if...? What if Microsoft ever abandons OneNote completely (don't panic! No signs of this)? What if you abandon MS Office or OneNote from whatever reason? What if a new government declares ONE- and ONEPKG files as illegal? Enough kidding, you get the point.

But wouldn't it leave a good feeling to have all your notes stored in a format that is completely independent of OneNote? If not to transfer them to another note program, then at least to keep all that valuable information in a readable form.

There is a way and format to do that: Export all your notes / notebooks to PDF files and store them away (you may even print them out and put the stack of paper in a safe). Here's how you do it:

1. Open the notebook you want to back up as a PDF and wait for it to completely load / synchronize.

2. Click on *File – Export*.

3. Under *Export Current,* select *Notebook*.

4. In the *Select Format* column choose *PDF*.

5. In the next dialog box, choose a destination drive and folder and start the export by clicking on *Save*.

The resulting PDF does not preserve the original note layout very well. Bigger (OneNote) pages may even be split into several PDF pages in a nonpredictable manner, but form follows function here. The important thing is that all your valuable content is safe, independent of the OneNote application and can be opened and read on any device or operating system.

 While files and documents stored in OneNote as printouts are preserved with this method, you will lose all files that have been embedded on notes. Their original icons show up in the PDF document, but those are just images.

Chapter 6   Shortcuts

When talking about software, the term "Shortcuts" is mostly used for pressing combinations of keys to avoid having to use the mouse. Well, some of those are introduced in this chapter too, but we also call it a shortcut to dig out commands and functions that are buried in the depths of the user interface. In addition, you'll learn to place shortcuts at a certain notebook location on the desktop and some command line parameters for OneNote.

93   Creating desktop shortcuts to notes

Each time you start OneNote, it loads the page you were on the last time you closed the program.

Maybe though you want a desktop shortcut or initial menu entry that starts OneNote and always opens to a certain page, section or notebook. You can do that very easily.

Right-click on the object you want to link to – which might be a page tab in the page tabs list, a section or section group tab at the top, or a notebook name. From the context menu, select the command to copy a link to this object into the clipboard. Depending on where you want to link to, the menu entry is named **Copy Link to Page**, **Copy Link to Section**, **Copy Link to Section Group** or **Copy Link to Notebook**.

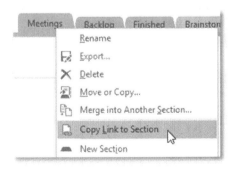

If the notebook you are linking to is stored in the cloud (OneDrive, OneDrive for Business), you now have two separate links in the clipboard. The link beginning with *http* opens the notebook, section or page in OneNote Online using the browser. The other link begins with *onenote: xxx* and loads that content into your locally installed OneNote 2013/2016 or the Windows 10 App. Usually you want your shortcut to use the second (local) link, so you need to remove the *http* link. This is how you do it:

1. Open Windows Editor (or another text editor) and paste the links from the clipboard into it. The result should look something like this:

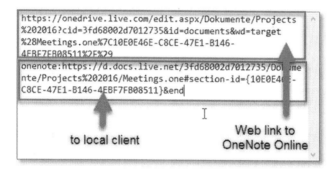

2. Select the second link, starting with *onenote:* and copy it to the clipboard with **[CTRL] + [C]**. Close the editor; you don't have to save the text file.

3. Now create a shortcut on your Windows desktop. Paste the link from the clipboard into the ***Type the location of the item*** field using **[CTRL] + [V]** and click on ***Next***.

4. In the next dialog box, you may want to replace the default name ***New Internet Shortcut*** with a more descriptive one of your choice.

94 Opening a page at Windows start

A useful addition to the previous desktop shortcut tip: If you want to open OneNote with specific content every time you boot up Windows, you can put a shortcut to a certain page, section or notebook into the Windows Startup folder.

This is the easiest way to access the startup folder in Windows versions 8, 8.1 and 10:

1. Press the keyboard shortcut **[Win]** + **[R]**.

2. Enter the command ***shell:startup*** into the ***Open:*** text-box and press **[Return]** or click on ***OK.***

The Startup folder opens in Windows Explorer. Now you just copy or move your desktop shortcut (as created in the previous tip) into it.

95 Pin a notebook to the Start menu

In Tip #93 you learned how to create a notebook, section or page link to put as a shortcut on the Windows desktop. How about having such a link as a tile in the Start menu of Windows 8 or 10?

Microsoft hasn't yet implemented an official way to create a Start menu tile based on a link or file. Using the context menu entry or drag and drop won't work either. It may well be this function will be added by a future Windows update. You don't have to wait for that. Just use the following trick (by the way. this works with all kinds of links and documents).

1. First you create a desktop shortcut to your notebook, section or page as described in Tip #93 .

2. Open your File Explorer and navigate to **C:\Pro-gramData\Microsoft\Windows\Start Menu\Programs**. This is the correct folder if you want all users of the computer to see the shortcut tile in their Start menu. If

you want to limit this to the current user, navigate to **C:\Users\User\AppData\Roaming\Microsoft\Windows\Start Menu\Programs** instead.

3. Now move or copy the desktop shortcut you created in step 1 to that folder. You need administrator rights for this action.

4. Open the Windows Start menu and look for your shortcut in the left apps list. If you haven't updated to Windows 10 1607 (Anniversary Update) yet, you would have to click on **All Apps** first.

5. Right-click on the app list entry of your OneNote shortcut and select **Pin to "Start"**. You're done.

96 Send or pass a link to a note

Sometimes you may want to point a friend or colleague to a certain page or paragraph in a note. Even if you shared the notebook with him, you would still have to tell him the correct paragraph and page so he could find that content. There is a much more convenient way though.

In the tip about creating a desktop shortcut (Tip #93), you learned how to create a link leading to a certain notebook, section, page or object within a page. That link may also be inserted in a chat message or E-mail. In most cases, you don't even have to separate the links for OneNote Online and the local client. In many programs both links get inserted side by side and the recipient may choose if he wants to open the note in the browser or in his locally installed OneNote client.

Some applications, for example Skype, don't interpret the second (local, beginning with "onenote:") link as a hyperlink, inserting it as plain text instead. In that case the recipient would have to select the complete link, copy it to the clipboard and either paste it into the URL input field of the browser or another editor (like MS Word or OneNote itself) to make it clickable.

 The prerequisite for this to work is that the recipient already has access to the corresponding notebook. Either it has been shared with him on OneDrive, SharePoint or OneDrive for Business or it is stored on a network location to which he has access rights.

97 Quick Note as a shortcut or at startup

You most likely already know how to open a new Quick Note using a keyboard shortcut (**[Win]**+**[N]**). What you may not know: There is even a command line parameter for starting OneNote in that "Quick Note mode".

This means you can create a desktop shortcut for taking a Quick Note or – even better – put that shortcut into the Windows startup folder so you always have a little note window at hand. Just put this into the **Type the location of the item** textbox of the new desktop shortcut:

Onenote.exe /sidenote

98   Start OneNote in docked mode

The docked mode of OneNote allows you to take notes on the side while working with another program like Microsoft Word. The OneNote window is shrunk to a small part of the screen, leaving the main part to the program you are working with. If that happens to be MS Word or Internet Explorer (sorry, Edge and other browsers are not supported...yet?), notes you take are even linked with the open webpage or the current text paragraph in Word.

Usually you start a docked OneNote window by selecting **New Docked Window** from the **View** menu. A little known fact is that there is a command line parameter that you could use in a desktop shortcut to directly start OneNote in docked mode. Just add "/docked" to "ONENOTE.EXE", for example:

"C:\Program Files (x86)\Microsoft Office\Office16\ONE-NOTE.EXE" /docked

Depending on the drive and folder where your MS Office is installed, you may have to change the path. "Office16" becomes "Office15" if you are using MS Office 2013.

99 Useful keyboard shortcuts

Like most Windows programs, you can control OneNote using keyboard shortcuts instead of using menus and mouse. In fact there are a lot of them. You find a complete listing by visiting

OneNote 2016:
https://support.office.com/en-us/article/Keyboard-shortcuts-in-OneNote-2016-for-Windows-44b8b3f4-c274-4bcc-a089-e80fdcc87950

OneNote 2013:
https://support.office.com/en-us/article/Keyboard-shortcuts-in-OneNote-2013-65DC79FA-DE36-4CA0-9A6E-DFE7F3452FF8

As those links are not easy to retype, you can just start an internet search using a phrase like this:
"OneNote keyboard shortcuts site:support.office.com"
Note that both versions of OneNote basically use the same shortcuts.

That list is very long, mainly because there are a lot of shortcuts included that apply to other Windows or Office applications. Let's pick a few shortcuts from the list that we find very useful in particular. Some of these are well worth memorizing.

[Crtl]+[M]: Create an additional OneNote window
Opens another OneNote window so you can view and edit several notes at once or move notes around more conveniently.

[Crtl]+[E]: Search
Sets the focus to the search field in the upper right and lets you enter a search term.

[Crtl] + [Shift] + [E]: Send current page via E-Mail
Creates a new mail message in your default mail client and inserts the current OneNote page. If you are using MS Outlook and HTML

message format is activated, the note content is displayed in its original layout. For other mail clients, a MHT file containing the note page is attached. To open the MHT file the recipient needs to use a browser that can read that file format (e.g. Internet Explorer).

[Return]: Open link
If the cursor is located somewhere inside an internal or external link, pressing the **[Return]** key doesn't start a new paragraph but opens that link in the browser or OneNote instead.

[F9]: Update (synchronize) all notebooks
Forces immediate synchronization of all opened notebooks.

[Crtl]+[F9]: Synchronize current notebook
Same as **[F9]** but limits the synchronization to the currently viewed notebook.

[Crtl]+[N]: Add a page
Same effect as clicking on *Add page* at the top of the page list.

[Alt]+[Cursor Left]; [Alt]+[Cursor Right]: Browse history
Browse back and forth in the history of recently viewed or edited pages. This history is erased when OneNote is closed.

[Crtl] + [Alt] + [L]: Lock protected pages
Immediately lock all currently unlocked, password protected pages.

[Crtl] + [Q] Mark page as unread
Displays the page title as bold and treats it as if it contains unread changes. May be used as a marker of sorts.

[Crtl] + [1] – [9]: Add or remove a tag
Shortcut to the first 10 tags. Can be used to add or remove a tag. You may change the order of the tags at any time to assign a spe-

cific keyboard shortcut. To do that open **Home – Tags – Custom-ize Tags**. In the following list use the little triangles at the top right of the list to move the selected entry up or down. The assigned keyboard shortcut is instantly shown.

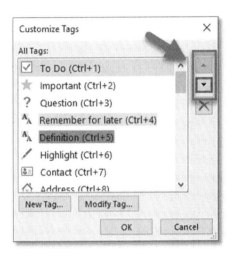

Insert date and time stamps:
[Alt] + [Shift] + [D]: Insert the current date.
[Alt] + [Shift] + [T]: Insert the current time.
[Alt] + [Shift] + [F]: Insert date and time stamp.

[Win] + [Alt] + [N]: Add a quick note
Create a Quick Note. OneNote doesn't need to be running for this to work.

100 Custom keyboard shortcuts

Most OneNote commands can be invoked using keyboard shortcuts. Usually they are displayed if you hover over a menu command and wait for the text in the tooltip to show up. Some of them are also shown in the previous tip. Unlike in other (Office) programs you cannot alter those shortcuts or define your own ones. There is just one exception - the Quick Access Toolbar (QAT).

Just like the commands on the ribbon, keyboard access to the Quick Access Toolbar always involves pressing the **[Alt]**-key. Press the **[Alt]**-key on its own to see key tips indicating these shortcuts. Activate the first command on the Quick Access Toolbar with keyboard shortcut **[Alt]** + **[1]**, the second command with **[Alt]** + **[2]** and so on until the ninth command with **[Alt]** + **[9]**.

From the 10th command button onwards, keyboard access is a bit more complex. Each keyboard shortcut starts with **[Alt]** + **[0]**, followed by an additional alphanumeric character. Combined with the 9 single-stroke keyboard shortcuts for the first 9 commands, this brings the total available number of keyboard shortcuts for the Quick Access Toolbar to 44.

- Command buttons 1-9: use **[Alt]** + **[1]** until **[Alt]** + **[9]**

- Command buttons 10-18: use **[Alt]** + **[0] [1]** until **[Alt]** + **[0] [9]**

- Command buttons 19-44: use **[Alt]** + **[0] [Z]** until **[Alt]** + **[0] [A]**

This means that by shifting the order of the commands on the Quick Access Toolbar, you can determine precisely which keyboard shortcut is to be used to access that command. Access the Quick Access Toolbar settings dialog box by opening *File – Options – Quick Access Toolbar*. Then change the order of the commands using the Move Up and Move Down buttons.

One more thing...

You have reached the end of the **OneNote Secrets**. We hope you have discovered a tip or two that really helped you to do more with OneNote 2013/2016, solved a problem or showed you a workaround for a missing function.

But wait! We have one more tip. Here it comes. It's not really about OneNote, but we are sure you will like it.

101 This book as a OneNote file

Can you think of a better format for a OneNote tips collection than OneNote itself? We thought so and put every tip from this book in a OneNote notebook. It's even available in two versions: As a OneNote Online notebook (read only) to be opened in a web browser and in addition as a ONEPKG-file (see Tip #88 to import it into your own OneNote 2013/2016, modify it and add content at will.

What does it cost? Nothing, except for a few minutes of your time. We are only asking you to leave a comment about the book on Amazon. After that just send a short e-mail to this address:

onenote-secrets@outlook.com

You will quickly receive an e-mail message containing an invitation link and instructions.

> **Important:** This offer is completely independent of the nature of your review on Amazon. Of course we also welcome critics if they help us to improve the next issue of OneNote Secrets. You will get the link regardless – promise!

10116526R00094

Made in the USA
Lexington, KY
18 September 2018